some of my best friends are people

SOME
OF MY
BEST FRIENDS
ARE
PEOPLE

by
art moger

CHALLENGE PRESS, INC.
Boston

Copyright, 1964, by Art Moger

SOME OF MY BEST FRIENDS ARE PEOPLE

For information address:

Challenge Press, Inc. 63 Summer Street, Boston, Mass.
Library of Congress catalog card No. 64–16413

First Edition

Dedicated to
My Wife, Dora
and children
Stan, Roz and Harriet—
without whose help this
book would have been
written—much sooner

(Any resemblance to persons, living or dead, is purely intentional.)

an explanation . . .

BY
EARL WILSON

(As practically dictated to him by art moger)

MOST BOOKS begin with an "Introduction." This one needs an "Explanation."

In the first place, the author is considered to be a good publicist. A noted cartoonist. A good family man. And a much sought-after, after-dinner speaker. Wherever he goes he is recognized. I once overheard a cabbie remarking to another driver as Moger crossed the street: "Hey, there goes whatsiz name!"

His rise to obscurity was blighted by his retentive memory for jokes and the ease with which he repeats them. This comes from a slogan he adopted early in life, "Lift and let lift!" He can hardly be called a plagiarist, since he maintains that "if you steal from one that is plagiarism. But if you steal from more than one it is 'research.'" Moger does a great deal of research, as you will soon find out.

Although the author wants you to think of this book as autobiographical anecdotes, it can hardly be termed a joke book. Moger leaves joke books to Bennett Cerf. Herein are many factual stories culled by Moger which happened to him as a reporter, movie publicist and cartoonist.

Among his little-known achievements is that he served as

a reporter for several Boston newspapers: *The Boston Post, The Boston Transcript, The Boston Globe* and *Herald-Traveler,* as well as the *Record-American-Sunday-Advertiser.* He has a BS in Journalism from Boston University. Now he has written this book?

If one story entertains you, as I'm sure many will, the price of the book is well worth what the publishers are asking for it.

Moger's nefarious career began when he was a grade school student. He wore long tresses until the fourth grade. Was he embarrassed? No! But you should have seen the red face of the boy who carried Art's books home from school.

As a veteran writer and illustrator of books, magazine and newspaper articles, he served as a gag writer for Groucho Marx and often appeared as a featured guest on Fred Allen's popular coast-to-coast radio program, "It's Town Hall Tonight." On the night of June 22, 1938 (that memorable evening when Joe Louis massacred the Teutonic Titan of fisticuffs, Max Schmeling) Moger's radio audience exceeded 50,000,000 listeners—greater than any that had ever listened to President FDR and his fireside chats. Was Moger that good? Hell, no, but it had started to rain in New York's Polo Grounds and the network announced that if the rain persisted it might have to move the fight into the Fred Allen spot. Moger's luck prevailed. It only sprinkled. Art became a celebrity and a nonentity overnight.

Movie premiers are synonymous with Moger. Wherever and whenever a new motion picture is launched, its star is usually accompanied by Art. Some of his printable experiences with the movie stars are related herein. He once wrote a book dealing with the best in radio, titled, *You'll Dial Laughing.* It was a noble experiment. Profits were donated to the Army Emergency Relief Fund. The book proved to be Hitler's secret weapon.

Records reveal that his draft board had him listed as "Isabel Moger." If WACS were ever recruited Art would have been the first to go.

During the world premier of *Giant*, he was called in to serve as 'Liz Taylor's bodyguard. An enviable chore, to say the least.

This brings me to a touchy subject . . . an embarrassing one which is revealed here for the first time. Art states that due to my ethical writings I "saved" the day for 'Liz Taylor, Mike and Warner Bros.' investment of more than $8,000,000 for *Giant*. This, like most of the stories Art writes about, is as sacrosanct as peeping through a keyhole and seeing another eye looking back at you.

The secret of Moger's success, if you can call it that, is that he has a penchant for starting something and not quite finishing it. It is commonly known that he experimented with a soft drink and called it's secret ingredients "One-Up." Further developments in its formula resulted in changing its name to "Two-Up," "Three-Up," "Four-Up," and "Five-Up." Moger stopped at "Six-Up." You all know what happened when the next guy came along where Moger left off.

I have been told that Art wasn't the smartest kid in school, but he was the best dressed. He was the only one in his class with his own Stetson dunce cap. Later he grew some (or is it gruesome) and developed a remarkable resemblance to Frankie Fontaine, Toots Shor, David Dubinsky, Bob Hope and a coterie of other notables. All of them have denied kinship.

Once Groucho Marx asked Art to leave Boston and relocate in Hollywood, where Groucho's cast of fellow writers, Arthur Sheekman, Tom MacKnight and Nat Perrin would join him. Moger refused the offer. Many years later, Groucho ran into Moger in Boston. His greeting to Art was, "Schmuck, are you still here? I thought they would have barred you from Boston by now!"

Maybe that's why I refer to him as "The Bard of Boston." Occasionally, my column will carry a one-liner from Art like: "I can't watch Mickey Mouse because he gives me Disney spells," or, "All television medicine shows should be shown on a spectacular called: 'Of Human Bandage'!" As the above proves conclusively, Moger has trouble separating the chaff from the wit.

As a person, Moger is not all bad. He has a great personality, a great talent, a great sense of humor, a great driving quality and a great capacity for work. As a matter of fact, he's so *great*, he starts to *grate* on your nerves.

I deem it a personal pleasure to write this introduction for *Some Of My Best Friends Are People*. I consider Art a good friend. There's nothing I wouldn't do for him and I know there is nothing he wouldn't do for me. That's exactly how it's always been between us . . . we've done exactly *nothing* for each other.

FOREWORD

To Art.—one of my Best Friends —

This foreword is written without my having seen the book it is the foreword to. So I don't know anything about the book; but I do know the author, and that's what this will be about.

I have known Art Moger for thirty years. In that time, he has publicized public figures who haven't half the charm he has; he has tried to whomp up enthusiasm for comedians who aren't half as delightful as he is; he has beaten the drum for movies, which seldom told stories comparable to those Art could tell.

In a town like Boston, where public relations men seem to have learned their profession at embalming schools, Art is an oasis. He has all the flair of the Hollywood guys, without their fawning fraudulence; he has all the vitality of the New York guys without their noisy manners.

I'm always glad to see Art. No matter how little quality the thing he's publicizing has, *he* has a quality that makes him a joy to see.

And to read, too, I'll bet.

PART ONE

name dropper

> *Hollywood is a place where your best friend will plunge a knife in your back and then call the police to tell them that you are carrying a concealed weapon.*
>
> —George Frazier

FOR THE LOVE OF MIKE—A TAYLOR–MADE TALE

A TEMPERAMENTAL movie star is ninety per cent *temper* and ten per cent *mental*. If you think this is just a show biz cliché, let me tell you about Elizabeth Taylor.

It was at the world premiere of *Giant* at the Roxy Theater on Broadway. I was assigned by Warner Bros. as her bodyguard. Mike Todd was her escort. (He had not released *Around The World In 80 Days,* and was still unknown as the great movie producer his academy award film was to make him.)

As 'Liz stepped from the chauffeur-driven limousine, the first thing I noticed were her eyes. Honest! They are a pale orchid hue instead of the customary blue, brown or hazel. I looked twice to make sure that my own bloodshot eyes weren't playing tricks.

1

Her decollete black silk, skin-tight gown revealed the deep cleavage of breasts out of proportion to her slight stature. Richard Burton's love inspired description is quite accurate:

"All this stuff about Elizabeth being the most beautiful girl in the world is absolute nonsense. She's a pretty girl, of course, and she has wonderful eyes; but she has a double chin and an overdeveloped chest and she's short in leg. So I can hardly describe her as the most beautiful creature I've ever seen."

As 'Liz and Mike entered the Roxy Theater, a Warner Bros. executive shoved me in their direction. I introduced myself—amid the shrieks and incoherent jabbering of the unruly crowd.

"Fer Chris' sake, if it ain't *The Kid From Boston*" greeted me. Mike Todd grinned, trying to hold onto 'Liz as the crowd surged upon us. They had come to see their screen heroine, Elizabeth Taylor! Many of them were determined to *feel* as well as *see*. Mike and I joined hands trying to protect her.

A woman fell in front of us. Mike tried to hold back the enthusiastic movie fans. "Stop! Stop! There's a woman on the ground," he shouted. "She'll be trampled to death! Stop, I say! Stop!"

"Art," he screamed at me, "whereinhell can we get away from this mob? We'll all be killed!"

Just inside the lobby I spotted a door and pushed 'Liz and Mike through it. It was an electrician's booth.

Two electricians were standing by a panel board, waiting to douse the house lights so that the film could begin.

"Where the hell is the booze?" Mike demanded. "Can't you see that 'Liz is all shook up?"

Liz looked frightened. She was shaking like an aspen leaf. Her hair was in a state of disarray and her gown was torn at the shoulder.

"We don't have any booze here."

"For God's sake, Art, run out and get me a bottle of Scotch," Mike said, still puffing.

Fortunately, I found a package store near the theater. With torn tux and hair askew I rushed back with the bottle. Mike poured a stiff drink for all of us. He then poured another double jigger for 'Liz. She drank it down without a chaser. He plied her with a third shot and then a fourth. Her composure regained 'Liz combed her hair, straightened out her dress and turned to Mike and said: "I guess we ought to go in and see the picture, Mike, dear."

Todd handed me 'Liz's ermine wrap. "You stay here, Kid. Liz doesn't know it but we aren't staying for the whole picture. I got other things on my mind." He winked.

The lobby was deserted. Everyone had gone into the theater except for a distraught woman who grabbed Mike. "Are you the manager?"

"Yes, I am," said Mike. "Wassamatter?"

"You just look at my shoes. One of them is a black one and the other is a brown one. I lost a black one when I fell down in the crowd as you came in."

"Come back after the show, lady," Mike chuckled. "Someone will notice the same mistake and turn back your shoe."

Mike grabbed 'Liz's arm and they both disappeared into the orchestra. The film had already been on for about half an hour.

About thirty minutes later Mike and 'Liz, followed by a group of press agents and Roxy attendants, rejoined me in the electrician's booth where I was finishing the bottle and snoozing on 'Liz's ermine wrap. Mike was swearing.

"You shouldn't have said that, Mike," 'Liz said angrily. "Not in front of him. He'll print it and it will ruin the whole premiere!"

"If he prints one damned word I'll sue him for every damned nickel he's got, and that goes for his paper, too."

Squeezed between them in the tiny room I tried to guess what happened. "Do you know Earl Wilson, Art?" Mike asked, his face beefy red.

"Sure I do. Every once in a while he uses a little one-liner, a gag which he pins on me. He nicknamed me the 'Bard of Boston.' Why?"

"Liz thinks he's gonna write something terrible in his damned column!"

Liz pouted, "Mike said that we were leaving because he had seen enough of me on the screen."

"What did Earl say?"

"Oh, something about 'Wassamatter, Miss Taylor, can't you take your own acting?' "

"All right," Mike grinned, "I admit it was my fault. I nudged 'Liz a couple of times and told her let's get the hell out of here and go back to the hotel. I didn't want to hang around and see a movie for two hours when we could be doin' somethin' else more useful." Mike gave me a poke.

"Be a good guy, Art, and see that Wilson doesn't make any sly innuendoes in his damned column."

I didn't wait for him to finish. I dashed for the lobby. Out of sight, I walked slowly towards the men's room and waited a few minutes and then returned to the electrician's booth. Mike opened the door cautiously. "Didja see Wilson? What did he say?"

"Nothing to worry about," I said, crossing my fingers.

"Are we going to stay trapped here until the picture is finished?" 'Liz demanded.

"Hell, let's go back and see the end of the movie," Mike said.

"Are you insane? We can't go back now. Earl will think you didn't dare go back to the hotel. What am I going to do crushed in here for half an hour?"

4

"Why don't you go to the can and read a funny book," Mike chuckled taking another drink.

"Do you know what in hell you are saying, Mike?"

"Why not? You know you say something brilliant every time you take your head out of a comic book. Okay, to hell with it, let's go back to the hotel and freshen up for the party at the Harwyn Club that Warners is throwin' for you. Gimme 'Liz's wrap, Art. See ya at the Harwyn Club in about an hour. You certainly came through for me. I won't forget it, Kid. By the way, did you ever get paid from that flop show I had in Boston, *The Man From Cairo?* I owed ya some dough for some ads and cartoons, didn't I?"

I assured him that I did get my money. *The Man From Cairo* was a flop. To get my money I had to have a lawyer attach the box office at the Wilbur.

"You lucky sonovabitch. You were the only bastard who got paid from that show!"

I returned to my hotel. I couldn't sleep. I waited for the *Post* to make its appearance on the street. Would Earl Wilson make a liar out of me? Would he *really* tell why 'Liz and Mike left the *Giant* premiere before the end of the picture?

I bought the *Post.* Nervously I turned to "It Happened Last Night" by the self-appointed Saloon Editor, Earl Wilson. I have a faded copy beside me. It reads:

"Before the premiere of *Giant* was over, 'Liz Taylor left with Grandpa Mike Todd for a party at the Harwyn. 'Here's why 'Liz left early,' Mike explained. 'All the broads in town who are crazy about me were waiting there to get my autograph and I was afraid they'd cause a riot and crush their feet. So I got 'Liz out before she got hurt by *my* fans.'"

First lesson in press-agentry. Take a chance . . . but cross your fingers and pray!

IT ALL STARTED out as a gag . . .

"They're all asking me what I am doing in Boston?" said lovely movie star Alexis Smith, as beautiful a woman as you'd ever want to see.

"Well, what ARE you doing in Boston?" I asked.

"To tell you the truth, I don't know myself. I'm under suspension from Warner Bros. because I refused to talk to a horse. My agent asked me to come here to make a guest appearance at the annual Jefferson-Jackson Day dinner at the Hotel Statler Saturday night. He didn't tell me what the committee wanted me to do."

At that moment, as though it were prearranged, three stalwart Democrats came into Miss Smith's suite.

"We have you on the program to sing the Star Spangled Banner, then you sing again after the first speaker, then later you'll sing . . . ," began one of the politicians.

"Wait a minute, gentlemen," said the movie actress. "I left my singing voice and red wig back in Hollywood after I completed *St. Louis Woman.* I don't sing at all!"

They looked at one another in awe. They gasped in horror to think that they had made a two thousand dollar commitment to bring a movie star to their greatest annual political event, only to find out that her singing voice had been "dubbed."

"B-but what will you do?" they asked in unison.

"Don't be panicky," I replied. "Leave me alone with Miss Smith for about an hour. Come back and we'll have the whole thing straightened out."

They left, and I sat down with a perplexed Alexis.

Having been a gagwriter for such diversified talent as Bob Hope, Groucho Marx and Fred Allen, I knew that suc-

6

cessful scripts need a good beginning and a close. You can always fill in the "middle" with something.

I thought and thought . . . and thought. And then . . . inspiration!

"Here's all you have to do, Alexis. "Begin by telling them the truth: Everywhere I go, people are asking me What's Alexis Smith doing at a Jefferson-Jackson Day dinner? I know of no better place that I should be than HERE with all of you fellow-Democrats at this fine Jefferson-Jackson Day dinner, because, after all, my real name is 'AL' Smith!"

Alexis took it from there sans song!

PAGING "THE THIN MAN!"

IT WAS A SURPRISE to me when Warner Bros. selected Springfield, Massachusetts as the center of the world premiere activities for *Springfield Rifle,* a historical drama of the Civil War in the West.

Only a few weeks before one of the top executives supposedly rushed up to the ticket seller at a railroad station and shouted: "Give me a ticket to Springfield!" "There are many Springfields in the U.S.A.," replied the ticket seller. "Which one do you want? Springfield, Illinois, Ohio or Massachusetts?"

"It makes no difference. Which costs cheaper?"

So, when I was told that I would head up a group of Hollywood celebrities, including Phyllis Kirk, David Brian, Guinn "Big Boy" Williams and his pretty wife, Florence, I made the necessary arrangements for hotel accommodations and the festive activities that would stimulate the kickoff of this technicolor film. A call was left for all the members of this Hollywood entourage to meet with me and my associate, Joe Friedman, in the lobby of the Sheraton-Kimball Hotel at 7:30 A.M. for an inspection of the famous Springfield Armory. This wasn't easy to arrange since the Armory was engaged in the manufacture of highly secret weapons. My good friend the then Mayor Daniel Brunton, made it possible. The Armory visit meant a good deal of local newspaper coverage.

At the designated hour, all were waiting in the lobby with the exception of the female star of the film, Miss Kirk. I sent Joe to the house phone but no one responded to the constant ringing.

While I held the phone, Joe went to Phyllis' room and rapped a few times, soft at first, then bang, bang! Still no answer. He could hear the telephone ringing continuously with that lonesome loudness that can give one the chills.

"I think she's not in her room," said Joe.

We canvassed the dining room and checked with the desk clerk as to Miss Kirk's whereabouts. No one had seen her that morning. We had all come in together at an early hour the night before. There isn't much doing in Springfield after ten.

I went up to Miss Kirk's room and started banging on her door again. The noise was loud enough to wake up four or five residents on the same floor. But, as for Miss Kirk . . . no answer!

An ideal spot for the "Thin Man."

I sent for a locksmith. After much fussing and lock-breaking we entered the room. And there was this petite figure curled up, covered with a bed sheet, her head right next to the telephone which was still ringing.

"She's dead!" shouted Joe.

I could see the newspaper headlines: "HOLLYWOOD ACTRESS DIES BEFORE FILM PREMIERE." Springfield would become known the breadth of our land, yes. First, "where a movie star had died." Second, "the home of the Springfield rifle." And, for us, that was the wrong order of importance.

I walked over to Miss Kirk and shook her.

She jumped up, and the sheet fell to her knees. She stared at me, glassy-eyed grabbing for the bed sheet to cover herself.

"Get out of here! What are you doing here? Help! Help!"

We tried to pacify her as best we could. Finally, she became rational and asked if we would please leave so that she could get dressed.

In less than five minutes she was in the lobby of the hotel as wide awake as any of us, wearing high black gloves, and ready for the tour of the Springfield Armory.

"Gosh! I certainly am a sound sleeper," she remarked as we stepped into a waiting cab.

An understatement if I ever heard one.

MEET "MISS TITLE"

ONE OF THE easiest ways to crash a newspaper and get voluminous space is to get a photograph of a shapely miss and name her "Miss Somethingorother."

It was with this thought in mind that I persuaded a newspaper editor to run a feature story about an up-and-coming actress named Janis Paige. To this day she is known by the title I bestowed on her many years ago.

You all know Frank Sinatra as "The Voice," Betty Grable as "The Legs," Jayne Mansfield as "The Bosom" and Marie McDonald as "The Body." These are all press agent gimmicks. There are even girls with such odd titles as "Miss Virgin Chinchillas," "Miss Dill Pickles," "Miss Orange Marmalade," and sundry screwier publicity handles.

Janis was the most titled girl in the world and was given her fifty-eighth title by me . . . "Miss Front Paige." What could be more appropriate?

She had hoped that this would symbolize her among the

Hollywood "greats" as a title-holder, not unlike Princess Grace.

Here are some of the honors heaped upon her, with and without her permission. She had been everything from "Miss Delicious Apples" to "Miss Best Table Decoration." She's been sponsored by everybody from bellhops to dam builders. Her name is plastered on the shiny nose of a transport plane and there's even a horse with her moniker pounding the eastern tracks.

In Washington D.C., bellhops rallied and voted her "the girl we'd like most to Paige." Corny?

Janis is a gorgeous hunk of dame who gets a kick out of receiving titles and maybe she has something to do with it, too.

"It's been good luck for me because my first title was "Miss Hollywood Canteen," she explained. "I got that when I substituted for another starlet at the Hollywood Canteen when I first went to California.

A talent scout spotted her and since then she's been piling up motion pictures, stage shows and television contracts almost as fast as titles.

The title to end all titles was "Miss Wing Spread," bestowed upon her to commemorate the maiden flight of a new bomber.

Pretty apt!

CALL IT A DAY

DORIS DAY is a fine actress and a good singer, too.

I first met her when she was "discovered" by Michael Curtiz, the incoherent Hungarian Academy Award winning-director at Warner Bros. She was starring in her first, yet-to-be-released-film, *I'll See You In My Dreams*. Someone at the studio decided it would be a good idea to send her "on tour." Why not let her go out with Les Brown and his band of renown? After all, hadn't she made her first big hit record singing with his band, "Sentimental Journey"?

So it was decided by the big movie moguls that this would be a good showcase for her talents. They didn't believe that Curtiz had made such a good choice in this freckled, pug-nosed singer named Dorothy Kappelhoff from Milwaukee.

She'd get good coverage, the studio agreed, because the "star" of the show was none other than Bob Hope—America's number one comedian.

"Go ahead," they told me from the home office. "You'll be covering twenty-five cities in twenty-three days."

"But I don't like to fly," I said cautiously.

"What the hell do we care how you get to the different towns? Go by pogo stick. But be damned sure that you tell everyone about this gal Doris Day and her next picture for Warners."

I scheduled myself for a score of southern cities and neighboring towns . . . always trying to get ahead of the troupe which was flying in Hope's DC 7.

Finally, they caught up with me in Charlotte, S.C. My train arrived just in time for me to catch the gang at the airport.

"Hya, Artie-boy," shouted the buoyant Hope, as he got off the plane. "I want ya to meet the star of the show, Doris Day."

Bob showed me newspaper after newspaper clipping. "Dodo" as he called her had been given star billing. "After all," he said, "everyone knows me. But this little kid has real talent. She's gonna be a big star and I wanna be the first one to say 'I told ya so.'"

We were met at the airport by a group of Elks, who were sponsoring the outdoor jamboree which featured Bob, Dodo and the Les Brown band. When an Elk takes a drink he starts

11

to show his teeth. When a group of them drink, well they can be mighty dangerous, especially when they have a new car and have been sent to "escort" the pretty young lady back to the hotel.

"Dodo" refused to go alone with the high spirited Elks. She asked me to accompany her. She sat on my lap for almost twenty miles while the car filled with alcoholic Elks clipped along at sixty miles an hour.

I don't know if I made any impression on "Dodo" but she made one on me. My knees haven't been the same since.

MR. SCHINE . . . MEET MR. MELCHER!

PROMOTING THE OPENING of one of the nation's first airport motels, at Bradley Air Field near Hartford, Connecticut, I engaged a local press agent to help me. Hearing that Doris Day was to be making a film nearby, I called my aide and told him to tell her husband, Marty Melcher, that I wanted to take her picture, with due credits to her new film, to publicize the opening of the airport. (I had met Marty when he was a press agent for the Andrew Sisters singing trio.)

Supposedly, all was in readiness, until I went down to a little town called Thompsonville, where "Dodo" was starring in a film with Ernie Kovacs and Jack Lemmon.

I telephoned Marty and told him that I was in town and ready for the publicity picture.

"What publicity picture?" he demanded. "Some nut called me and told me that you would call me but that's all I know about 'Dodo' posing for a picture."

I hopped into my car and went looking for Melcher. I finally located him at the railroad station. A train was slowly backing into the platform. A limousine came alongside the train. Out stepped Miss Day. I waved to her and beckoned: "Hy, Dodo, it's Art Moger, remember?"

12

But Dodo didn't remember her night on my lap. Eventually Marty came by. We exchanged greetings and I told him that David Schine was building a new airport hotel. Since the movie company was nearby it would be a good publicity shot. (For me, at least).

"Dave Schine?" he exploded. "Why that character wouldn't do anyone any good. I wouldn't give him the right time. Forget it!"

"Dave's not looking for the right time," I pleaded. "Just one little picture of Dodo and Mr. Schine, please, Marty! Just one little picture!"

"Forget it. If you think that I'm going to jeopardize a free tieup I have with the New York, New Haven Railroad for the use of its trains to publicize an AIRPORT hotel, you must be crazy!" he shouted.

Marty started to walk away as the train pulled out. I got into my automobile with Mr. and Mrs. Schine (she was a former Miss Universe winner) and raced to meet the train at the other end of the station. It was reminiscent of a Mack Sennett chase. Slamming on the brakes we arrived at the other end of the train. But it didn't stop. It backed to where we had started from. We sped alongside of the train and finally arrived at the other end. Dodo stepped out onto the platform.

My cameraman was behind me. I rushed Mr. and Mrs. Schine out to meet her. "Shoot!" I shouted. He flashed his camera. Then I saw Marty Melcher come running towards me.

We shoved Mr. and Mrs. Schine into the car and drove them to their private plane which they had "parked" in an adjacent lot owned by a local farmer. Marty gave up the pursuit.

Eventually, the publicity picture appeared in newspapers throughout the country. We superimposed the Schine airport hotel in the back. A little retouching here and there and we had our publicity photo.

Sometimes even publicity men have to "stoop to conquer."

NO REQUIEM FOR DANNY KAYE

DANNY KAYE is a very tempermental performer. He has a phobia about having anyone touch him or his clothes.

When I toured with him to Toronto, on behalf of the fund-raising for a new hospital sponsored by the Variety Club, to be called "Variety Village," I came to the conclusion that he could easily have entered the diplomatic service of our country. Danny is intelligent and understanding. He's also impetuous.

One of the owners of the Prince George Hotel in Toronto, a fellow named Smith, asked Danny if he'd be his guest at his nightclub. Mr. Smith and his brother are now in a Canadian jail "sitting it out" for some stock swindle. They also were involved in the Havana Riviera, a gambling casino which Castro took over.

Reluctantly, Danny said he'd go, on the condition that no one introduce him from the floor and try to make a spectacle of him. Both his manager, Eddie Dukoff and myself cautioned Mr. Smith and it was agreed that Danny would just be a guest.

We entered the "upholstered sewer"—a smoke-filled, dingy club and quickly went to a table where we were seated. Danny ordered "breakfast" and we looked around us. The place was packed with Saturday night "spenders." A comedian was going through a routine, which was funny and dirty, too.

Danny made some comment about "that fellow could be a big star if he cleaned up his material. He has lots of talent and drive."

14

This was the first meeting I had with Red Buttons.

When the comedian finished his act, he said:

"—and now ladies and gentlemen, I want to introduce to you the greatest entertainer both continents have ever known . . . the one and only Mr. Danny Kaye. . . ."

The applause was deafening.

Danny turned to me and mumbled: "That dirty louse promised me he'd not introduce me. Why that dirty, two-timing sonavabitch. . . ."

I nudged Danny to stand up and take a bow as the electrician sent a light towards our table. Danny stood up and mumbled some inaudible epithets. He quickly sat down.

As he was about to put a forkful of eggs into his mouth (he is a very small eater, at irregular hours) a drunk sitting next to me leaned over to Danny and said:

"Fer C'rist sakes, whyinhell don'cha stand up and sing a song fer us? You goddam Americans are all alike. You come here and take away our dough and don't do a damn thing for us. . . ."

Danny leaned over me and addressed the drunk: "Sir, won't you come to my table and I'll explain to you why I won't sing. . . ."

The drunk rose tipsily from his table and started towards ours. Eddie Dukoff, a mild fellow of slim proportions who would faint if a marshmallow was tossed in his direction, saw the inebriate staggering towards Danny.

Sid Garfield, now a CBS executive and then a Warner Bros. publicist who had come to Canada to obtain some column "plants," alerted Eddie that "something was going to happen."

Eddie intercepted the drunk and pushed him backwards. The drunk was built like a well-dressed weight lifter or a ditch-digger.

I hastily grabbed (an unpardonable sin . . . to touch Mr.

Kaye) Danny by the sleeve and dragged him out into the lobby of the club.

"Whatinhell has come over you?" he shouted nervously. "Didn't you hear me ask that man to come to our table? Why did you push me out here?"

"Look, Danny," I replied, "what good is it going to do you or anyone to get into a discussion with a drunk. Even if you are right, what will it prove and to whom?"

Before he could answer me, a lady came out of the Powder Room in the lobby. She turned to Danny and said:

"You ARE Danny Kaye, aren't you?"

"I am," bowed Danny, graciously.

"I think you stink!" she muttered.

"You are not alone," replied Danny. "But I'm curious as to why you say that, ma'am."

"Well," she answered, "I was in the room a few minutes ago when they applauded and whistled when your name was mentioned. As a matter of fact, I applauded until my hands hurt. The least you could have done was go on the stage and sing a coupla songs for us."

Danny then started to explain how he needs special material, how he isn't a stand-up comedian like Bob Hope or Danny Thomas; how he was invited as a guest and not as a performer; how embarrassing it was to him, etc. He convinced not only the lady but me, too. This was exactly what he would have told the drunk. I'm sure his charm and sincerity would have won over the most cynical skeptic.

Suddenly, Mr. Smith and our group, consisting of Sid Garfield, Eddie Dukoff, Babe Koval and Haskell Masters, general manager of the WB for the Dominion of Canada, came running out into the lobby.

Smith was the first to speak: "Let's get out of here fast!"

"What happened?" I asked him.

"Jesus," Smitty said, "the guy that Eddie tangled with is a bad actor. Did you notice he had a half-filled bottle of Scotch on top of his table?" This is 'verboten' in all nightclubs. I could lose my license for that. About a week ago, this guy was released from a Federal Prison. He got into a fight with another mobster in my club a few nights ago, picked up a bottle of Scotch which was standing on his table, broke it and pushed the jagged edges into the other guy's face. He's out on bail, now. The other guy is in the hospital, disfigured and dying."

Danny Kaye might not have talked his way out of that one!

"SAYONARA" MEANS "GOODBYE"

SHE WAS A lovely oriental lady. Her name was Miiko Taka. She had the feminine lead opposite Marlon Brando in *Sayonara*, which won an Academy Award for comedian Red Buttons, and catapulted her to screen fame.

I first met her in Buffalo. She was bedecked in a colorful Japanese kimono, an obi and sandals. She looked like something out of a Japanese calendar or travel poster. As a matter of fact, she won her role in this film when her husband, a movie agent, took her for a trip to the set where Joshua Logan was casting for *Sayonara*. One look at her and Logan signed her on the spot for the much sought after role. She had never acted before in a movie film.

I introduced myself. She was accompanied by her sister-in-law.

"Hello, Art-Sun," she said.

"What's this 'Art-Sun' business?" I asked.

"Oh, the Japanese add the word sun at the end of a name. It's an endearing term. Like you say Yankkeleh or Izzaleh in Yiddish," said Miss Taka.

17

I looked at her and said: "Are you sure that your real name isn't 'Zelda Shapiro'? I think you must have had your eyes slanted and nose 'fixed' so that you'd get this role!"

She burst into laughter. "Funny you should say that. Danny Kaye calls me a 'Jupe' too."

"What's a 'Jupe'?" I asked.

"Oh, that's a Japanese Jew," she said.

I observed her unusual sandals and two-toed white socks. "Don't you ever trip on those sandals?"

"Never. I'm used to them. I wear them all of the time."

As we started to go down the hall, she fell flat on her nice plump obi.

Later that evening I asked her what her future plans were.

"I don't know," she answered. "If I never play another part in motion pictures I'll always feel that I could never top my role in *Sayonara*." She was right. However, since we had been kidding I suggested: "You'd be a natural for the lead in *Marjorie Morningstar*."

"Funny thing, that's what Danny Kaye said when I saw him last in Hollywood. I think I'd be good too."

She convinced me that Danny was right. Maybe she was a 'Jupe.'

The next morning I escorted Miiko and "Mary" to the airport. They were scheduled for a personal appearance in Cleveland where another press agent was meeting them. Miiko kissed me "Sayonara" or "goodbye." I'll always remember that kiss. I went home that night and was confined to my bed for a full week. The doctor's diagnosis: "Asian Flu."

FOR RICHARD OR POORER!

WHEN NEW YORK press agents come to Boston with a tryout show, they usually hire me to handle the local engagement. Such was the case when I squired Richard Rodgers around to help plug a play on which he had collaborated with Oscar Hammerstein II for the first time.

The play was called: "Away We Go."

We had just come back from an interview on radio station WNAC. Ruth Moss, a talented and charming interviewer, had wrung out of the shy Mr. Rodgers the fact that the Theatre Guild would rise or fall with the success of this musical production, the first in the Guild's history since *The Garrick Gaieties*, produced almost a quarter century previously.

Coming back in a taxi, Mr. Rodgers said to me:

"Here I am a songwriter with everything at stake. If this show is a flop, it's the end of the Theatre Guild and might make a great difference in my way of life. As I look back, I had a great future with Harry Kalmus, the pioneer of Technicolor films. My daughter, Mary, is a great student of the piano, so what? I'm sure I would have had plenty of security if I had only stuck with Harry. Today, look at Kalmus and the great success he has achieved in the motion picture industry! Everywhere you go, you see technicolor films. Sometimes I'm sorry I ever left him."

Just as we stepped out of the cab, Dick turned to me and said: "If you know anyone with a couple of thousand dollars to invest in this play, let me know. We're looking for some backers. It's a risk, you understand."

You have probably seen "Away We Go." It was renamed *Oklahoma*.

Poor Richard!

"HELLO, DAH–LINGS!"

TALLULAH BANKHEAD toured New England in a summer play called: "Welcome Darling." It is well known that she is not the easiest actress to get along with. Hence, when manager John McEvoy of the Somerset Playhouse sought someone to

19

"help" Miss Bankhead on and off the stage due to blinding lights and her own myopic condition, he found no takers.

Finally an elderly millworker asked John if he could have the job. He learned how to lead her on and off the stage. He also learned how to unzip her dress in short order so that she could make the quick changes she needed.

He loved "show business" and his duties were performed to milady's satisfaction. When the week's engagement was over, Tallulah called in McEvoy and said:

"Dah-ling you are simply wonderful. You are mah-velous! You gave me the most wonderful bitch I ever had in my life to help me on with my dress and lead me on and off of the stage. That sixteen year old deah was simply divine, dah-ling! Simply divine!"

"Sixteen years old?" recalls John. "Why that old bastard was nearer fifty. Tallulah never got a good look at him. Between the strong lights and her own nearsightedness I don't think she ever did see him! She should have known that a sixteen year older couldn't smell sweat as bad as that guy did!"

MELTING THE POT

ONE AFTERNOON last year, a young actor named Louis Morelli walked into an office in Hollywood. When he walked out, his name was Trax Colton. No one had ever heard of him before, and no one has heard of him since. But he has at least taken his minor place in an ancient rite of Hollywood. Moreover, Morelli was restyled by one of the wizard name changers now practicing the craft—Agent Henry Willson, the man who turned Marilyn Louis into Rhonda Fleming, Francis McGowan into Rory Calhoun, Arthur Gelien into Tab Hunter, Robert Moseley into Guy Madison, and—his great

Jayne Mansfield

Harry Belafonte

mind wandering from the New Jersey Palisades to the Strait of Gibraltar—Roy Fitzgerald into Rock Hudson.

Since it is axiomatic in show business that the name is rewritten before the teeth are capped, hundreds of literary types like Willson have, over the years, flung into the air a confetti storm of phony names that have settled lightly but meaningfully on the American culture.

The largest group is the Readily Understandables. Issur Danielovitch lacks, well, euphony. So the name was shortened to Kirk Douglas. It is also understandable why Tula Ellice Finklea would want to change her name to Cyd Charisse, Frances Gumm to Judy Garland, Bernie Schwartz to Tony Curtis, Sarah Jane Fulks to Jane Wyman, Emma Motzo to Lizabeth Scott, Judith Tuvim to Judy Holliday, Doris Kappelhoff to Doris Day, Aaron Chwatt to Red Buttons, Zelma Hedrick to Kathryn Grayson, Eunice Quedens to Eve Arden, Natasha Gurdin to Natalie Wood, Barney Zanville to Dane Clark and William Beedle to William Holden. England's James Stewart, eclipsed by Hollywood's James Stewart, changed his name to Stewart Granger. Frederick Bickel —rhymes with pickle—changed his name to Frederic March. Frederick Austerlitz was just too hobnailed a surname to weight the light soles of Fred Astaire. Cary Grant, of course, would have been unstoppable with any name from Pinky Fauntleroy to Adolf Hitler—even, for that matter, with his own name: Archie Leach.

But the whys start colliding with the wherefores. There is a group, for example, that could be called the Inexplicables. Why would a girl with a graceful name like Harriette Lake want to change it to Ann Southern? John F. Sullivan could have hardly been afraid of being mistaken for John L. when he changed his name to Fred Allen. The name Edythe Marrener is at least as interesting as Susan Hayward. Why change Thelma Ford to Shirley Booth, Jeanette Morrison to Janet Leigh, Patrick Barry to Barry Sullivan, Edward Flanagan to Dennis O'Keefe, Kim Reid to Kim Stanley, Virginia McMath to Ginger Rogers, Julie Wells to Julie Andrews, Helen Beck to Sally Rand, John Hamilton to Sterling Hayden, Diane Belmont to Lucille Ball, Phyllis Isley to Jennifer Jones?

Actors with plain, pronounceable, American Legion sort of names yearn for toning up. Ruby Stevens is Barbara Stanwyck; Peggy Middleton is Yvonne De Carlo; Norma Jeane Baker was Marilyn Monroe. Even Gladys Smith found a little more stature in the name Mary Pickford. On the other hand, embarrassed bluebloods shed their hyphens and thus declare their essential homogeneity with the masses. Reginald Truscott-Jones was too obviously soaked in tallyho. He became Ray Milland. Spangler Arlington Brugh denuded himself of all his nominal raiment and emerged as Robert Taylor. Audrey Hepburn-Ruston amputated it neatly.

Some real names are out of character. Roy Rogers was Leonard Slye. Boris Karloff could not have frightened a soul as William Henry Pratt. Gypsy Rose Lee has done things that Rose Louise Hovick would presumably never do. Other real names seem to be struggling to express themselves. Merry Mickey Rooney was once Joe Yule, Jr. Sam Goldwyn was Sam Goldfish. Shelley Winters was Shirley Schrift. Lili St. Cyr was Marie van Shaack. Diana Dors was Diana Fluck.

Hollywood stars come from every sort of ethnic and national-origin minority group. Many of them are bitterly vocal about U.S. democracy's failures. If enough of them had stuck by their original names, the resulting influence, through the vast popularity of the movies, would have done much to soften bias and reduce prejudice. No one would challenge their actions individually, but they could have served themselves better as a group.

Among actors of Italian and Spanish background, for example, Dino Crecetti opted it to be Dean Martin. Margarita Cansino became Rita Hayworth, Anna Maria Italiano is now Anne Bancroft. Anglicizing their names, Anthony Benedetto became Tony Bennett and Giovanni de Simone became Johnny Desmond. Among Jews, Izzy Itskowitz probably needed to sandpaper that a bit; yet he stayed with a Jewish name: Eddie Cantor. But most — from Jerry Levitch (Jerry Lewis) to Nathan Birnbaum (George Burns), Emanuel Goldenberg (Edward G. Robinson), Pauline Levy (Paulette Goddard), Rosetta Jacobs (Piper Laurie) and Melvin Hesselberg (Melvyn Douglas)—have preferred the Anglo-Saxon angle.

Many actors sculpt their real names. Ethel Zimmerman clipped off the "zim." Vivian Hartley lost her "hart." James Baumgarner dropped the "baum." Grace Stanfields is now Gracie Fields. Uncle Miltie was once Milton Belringer. One letter made the difference for Dorothy Lambour. First names have a habit of turning into surnames. Benny Kubelsky changed his name to Jack Benny, Muni Weisenfreund to Paul Muni, Preston Meservey to Robert Preston.

Last names vanish: Arlene Francis Kazanjian, Maybritt Wilkens, Eddie Albert Heimberger. Some stars can't stand their first names. Leslie Hope and Harry Crosby went for a solid Bob and a charming, chiming Bing.

Loilta Dolores Martinez Asunsolo Lopez Negrette is now Dolores Del Rio. Marion Morrison probably thought his name sounded girlish so he changed it to John Wayne. Douglas Fairbanks was really Douglas Ulman. June Allyson was Ella Geisman. Tasmania's Estelle Merle O'Brien Thompson started her career as Queenie Thompson, outgrew that and became Merle Oberon. Yul Brynner goes around saying that his original name was Taidje Khan, Jr. of northern Asia, but he is probably Alfie Jones of Kansas City, Missouri, or something like that. No one has ever been able to pin him down about his background, not even his wives.

Meanwhile, Rip Torn, that bisyllabic symbol of absurdly phony Holywood names, is really Rip Torn. His father was Rip Torn, too.

A CASE OF "REEL" NAME DROPPING

SHE WAS BORN Tula Ellice Finklea. Her brother nicknamed her "Sid." When she joined the Ballet Russe she was tagged "Felicia Sidarova." This was subsequently changed to "Maria Estamano." After her marriage she became Mrs. Nico Charisse.

At the start of her screen career she took the name "Lily Norwood." MGM changed that to "Sid Charisse," until her mail all began: "Dear Sir." Finally she was billed as Cyd Charisse.

Now, you all know that Cyd Charisse is really Mrs. Tony Martin, whose real name is Alfred Morris. Will the "reel" Tula Ellice Finklea please not bother to stand up!

FAIR AND WARNER

WHEN THE 3-Dimension film craze was at its height (it lasted well into one picture), the prophetic Jack L. Warner, Executive Producer of Warner Bros. Pictures, prophesied that within two years "everyone would be carrying around a pair of 3-D glasses in his pockets, just as he does a fountain pen and a wallet." This rumor caused Polaroid stock to soar from that day on.

The first time I met J.L. or "The Colonel" as he was commonly called, was when I was notified from my New York office, on a Thursday, that the Colonel himself was coming to Boston with his son, Jack, his secretary, Billy Schaefer, and

Jake Wilk, Eastern Story Editor for the film company. Would I be sure to get them all tickets to see the Harvard-Yale game on Saturday? And a suite at either the Ritz-Carlton or the Statler and see that "the boss gets the best of everything." I was given the flight number and arrival time two days hence. The plane was due at noon. It gave me plenty of time to obtain two police escorts and a limousine to give "the ole man" the best show he had ever seen. After all, "The Messiah of the Motion Picture Industry" was coming and here was my chance to show him what a good man I was.

A month before I had obtained two tickets to the Harvard-Yale game, promising my son, Stan, that he and I would see his first big time football game. Stan and I were inseparable buddies. We had planned to make a day of this event which had been sold out many months in advance. Our seats were in the wooden stands, a temporary bleacher section erected for the capacity crowd. They were the best that my brother Nate could get from his Harvard Class allotment. I was grateful that I had them.

Now, all I had to do was try to get four more seats.

"If worse comes to worse," I told my twelve-year-old son, "you and I will have to give up the game. I'll give Mr. Warner two seats and try to get two more."

"What does Mister Warner mean to me?" he asked.

As he slowly got off the floor, I reminded him that "The Colonel" meant bread and butter and an occasional eclair.

I put in a call to my "friends" for extra tickets. Did you ever try to get tickets to a sell-out affair a few hours before the event?

I called and called and called. Then I decided to make the rounds of the newspaper offices and try to inveigle my sports writing friends to part with a pair of tickets. Price was no object.

The late Burt Whitman, sports editor of the *Boston Herald*, was sympathetic. "It so happens that my brother-in-law is sick and can't go to the game. I have two tickets in the special section of the Stadium reserved for old time football players only. You can have them for what they cost me. Twenty dollars each. (I have yet to meet a sports editor who ever paid to go to a sporting event.)

I paid him the forty dollars. Now, I had four tickets. I then cornered Dave Egan of the *Boston Record*. He listened to my tale of woe and offered two press tickets which I could have for nothing. He promised to send them up to my office.

Late Friday night it began to snow. My phone started to ring at home. Tickets that had been impossible to get fell from the sky. Messengers kept bringing me tickets from all sections of the city. Cash on the barrel head. Saturday morning free tickets to the Harvard-Yale game were on Moger. I gave away twelve pairs.

Colonel Dave Egan sent me the two gratis press tickets good for the press box admission as he had promised.

At least I had tickets for the boss man and his party. At the same time I was trying to get a hotel suite for the Warner entourage. This proved even more difficult than getting the Harvard-Yale tickets. I called my hotel friends. No one, but no one, would help me. It was impossible. Boston was jammed. People were sleeping as far away as Worcester.

I couldn't take "No" for an answer. I had to make a good impression on Colonel Warner. One false move and Warner's might have a new publicity man.

I pleaded with Bert Stanbro, managing director of the Statler-Hilton: "Look, Bert," I begged, "maybe there were times when I said I needed a room for Colonel Warner and the room was really for some character who had a broad in town. But this is for real! You must do something for me. I promise never to ask you again. Please!"

"What can I do, Art? I just don't have any rooms available.

But, I have an idea. My wife and my children are going visiting. We won't be back to the hotel until eight o'clock in the evening. You can use our suite in the hotel until eight Saturday night. Comes eight o'clock you must get out, because my family and I will be coming back. Does this help you any?"

I had no choice but to accept Bert's kind offer.

Bert had no objection to having the suite registered in the name of Colonel Jack L. Warner and party.

I was moronically slap-happy! I had done it! The suite was mine. I had the tickets to the game. I had the police and limousine ready to meet Warner at Logan Airport at eleven o'clock, Saturday morning.

My son and I arrived at the airport in the hired limousine at ten-thirty. The temperature was eight degrees above zero.

When the plane with the Warner party aboard finally arrived at two P.M., the police escort had politely deserted me. Down the ramp swaggering and jaunty came Jack Warner wearing a lightweight coat and pearl grey double-breasted vest. He looked like his publicity pictures, with a healthy California tan on his face. Tagging along behind him was a jaundiced-looking carbon copy of himself, his son, who immediately ran into the men's room.

When Jack, Jr. finally came out of the washroom we all piled into the limousine and headed for Harvard Stadium. There was no time to lose . . . the game was on!

As we headed down Memorial Drive, toward the Stadium, with no police escorts, the Colonel asked me: "Do you have the football tickets for us, laddie?"

I told him that I had four tickets. Two were with the old time players, former Harvard and Yale football stars (that was what Bert Whitman had told me). I also told him that I had two tickets for the press box, which Dave Egan had given me. I mentioned my two seats in the wooden stands.

"Where do you think I'll be the least conspicuous?" he asked Jake Wilk, who was with the Colonel and had come to Boston to catch the opening of *Decision of Christopher Blake,* a new play by Moss Hart.

"If I were you, Colonel, I'd take your son to the section where the old time football players are. I will sit in the press box with Billy Schaefer. I think you'll like meeting all those football greats.

"Good," the Colonel said. "Let's synchronize our watches. We'll all meet back in the 'limo' at four-seventeen P.M. no matter what happens." (I still can't understand why he couldn't have made it four-fifteen instead of four-seventeen unless he had seen it in a James Cagney movie.) We all set our watches. Even Stan set his Mickey Mouse timepiece to coincide with the Colonel's expensive diamond-studded wristwatch.

As we passed Lever Brothers in Cambridge, the Colonel asked me if I could arrange to get him a few cases of soap, since it was quite a critical commodity during those war years. I assured him that I was friendly with "Chuck" Luckman, Lever's president, and could get him whatever he needed.

"I'm sailing for Europe in a few weeks. Have them deliver six cases to the *Queen Mary,* care of me."

"Dad," his son said, "I need some Lux Flakes for my apartment. Can you get me a case?"

"Granted, Jack, Jr.," I said.

We were approaching Harvard Stadium. The game was well into the first half.

Our chauffeur was instructed to keep the motor running and the heater on. It was bitterly cold outside. We parked near the clubhouse where a sign read "NO PARKING." What was a parking ticket in a crisis like this?

As I accompanied the Colonel to the Stadium, I glanced

28

at the tickets that I handed to him. They read: "Coliseum Section. East Tower."

Walking over to an usher I asked him where the section was located. He pointed up to the sky and said: "Way up there, Mister."

"Where's the elevator?" the Colonel demanded.

"Are you kiddin', mister? There is no elevator here. You gotta walk!"

I suddenly realized that I had been duped into believing that these forty dollar ducats were where the old time players were. Actually the seats were located somewhere in the path of the airplanes taking off from Logan Airport. The East Tower was in the direct path of the blizzard-like winds which were now blowing from all directions.

Two hours later numb with cold and minus five fingernails, I staggered back to the limousine with my son.

I opened the car door and was greeted with:

"Shut the goddam door!"

The Colonel rubbing his leg ignored me: "Oh, if I only can get the circulation back in my leg. Oh, my leg!" he moaned.

"How did you like the game?" I asked cheerfully.

"What game?" he demanded. "If you're the best manpower we have in the publicity department, I certainly don't think much of our field staff. There were no goddam seats to sit down on. There were no old-time players, unless they grew old as they climbed up those cement stairs. Every goddam freeloader I ever saw was there. Newsboys, shoe-shine boys, porters, and banner-sellers were there. Whereinhell did you you say you found these tickets?"

I turned to Jack, Jr. in the back seat and said: "Your dad's kidding, isn't he? How were the seats?"

"No, he isn't fooling. What he says is true. After climbing up all those friggin' stairs, we finally got our second wind before we froze to death and came back to the car."

"Whereinhell is Wilk and Shaefer?" whined J.L. "Jake Wilk knows this Stadium. Whyinhell didn't he give me those good tickets to the press box? Wait till he gets here. What's keeping him? It's already four-seventeen, right on the nose!"

About four-forty-five P.M. I saw two people, with coats on their sleeves, walking toward us. It was Jake Wilk and Billy Shaefer.

"Hya, boss," said Wilk, as he wiped off hot dog mustard stains from his sports shirt. "Boy, what a game! What seats we had, eh, Bill? Say, boss, we made connections with Bill Stern. He was in the press box near us. We're all set for the UCLA-Stanford game in California when we get back to Hollywood. That press box was so hot we had to sit around in our jackets."

Moger shuffled quietly into the doghouse, and licked his wounds. Worse was to come. I had forgotten the arrangements I had made for the Colonel's room.

When we arrived at the Statler, I walked up to the desk and asked for Colonel Warner's suite. It was waiting for us, just as Bert Stanbro had promised.

We went up to the room. Brandy was ordered for all of us. The Colonel continued to rub his left leg and stare ruefully at me. He stated categorically that he was literally frozen, through and through.

"Forget it, boss," Jake Wilk said admiring the room. "This is really cozy. It's like a home, not a hotel suite. Why don't we sleep over and take the first plane out in the morning. The last act of that play you want to see is the most important. You don't have to get the eleven o'clock plane. What do you say?"

I must have turned as white as a sheet.

"What's the matter with you, Art," the Colonel demanded. "Don't you feel well?"

"To tell you the truth, I don't, J.L.," I answered. "I think I'll take Stan home and come back."

"Before you do, call downstairs and get a dinner table for the five of us. Go home in the 'limo' and come back as soon as you can. We'll eat, then go to the theatre. I think Jake is right. I'll stay over."

I reached for the house phone and called Albert, the maitre d'.

"Get me a table for five, Albert. It's for Colonel Warner. I'll take care of you."

"But Mr. Moger," blurted Albert, "we have no room; the dining room is crowded."

"You have to do this for me, Albert," I pleaded.

"All right, Mr. Moger. But have your party come down right away. I'll have a table in your name. Don't wait too long!"

I took Stan home and rushed back to the hotel. What was I to do? If the Colonel decided to stay overnight, I was a cooked goose,—a dead duck. I had promised Bert Stanbro that I would get out of his private suite at eight P.M. sharp. No "ifs," "ands" or "buts."

Back at the hotel I went to the Terrace Room and searched for the Warner party. Albert told me that no one had shown up. He was holding a table for five, gave it up ten minutes ago. The dining room was jammed. I went up to Stanbro's apartment. The Warners, Wilk, and Shaefer were sitting around Stanbro's built-in kitchen . . . his "home."

"Cripes, they didn't have any reservation for us in the dining room!" the Colonel said disgustedly. "What the hell cooks?"

I found out they had gone to the Cafe Rouge instead of the Terrace Room and gave up in disgust when they couldn't get seated.

Warner then decided that he would order "room service" and mix his own special salad, from a studio recipe given to him by an old Frenchman. It was six-fifteen.

When the food finally arrived, he mixed the salad but added too much garlic and wound up with a slight gall bladder attack.

When we finally finished our meal, I looked at my watch and it was nearly seven-thirty.

"Have you heard the radio bulletins, Colonel," I said, praying softly he hadn't. "There's a rumor that we are due for the biggest blizzard in fifteen years. We'll be snowed in here for days."

"Good God, not that," the Colonel said. "Art, you better call the airport and tell them we want to get out of here by midnight. Here, take the plane tickets and change them for a midnight flight and don't flub these tickets."

I lost my nerve. How could I tell him that the last plane to New York from Logan was at eleven P.M. It looked as if the Colonel was going to miss the last act of Moss Hart's play even if it was the most important act.

I slowly walked back to the Plymouth Theatre and met J.L. who was talking to Moss Hart, the author of the play. I heard J.L. say to Mr. Hart: "Have you a shower in the theatre, Moss?"

"Why, er, I suppose so, Mr. Warner. Why do you ask?"

"Someone gave me one of these new-fangled ballpoint pens which write under water, so I thought you and I could make a deal for the movie rights to this play, now."

That was how *The Decision of Christopher Blake,* one of the movie's worst duds at the box office, was bought for $300,000 . . . even before the Colonel had seen the play, first, second and last act good or not.

"Why are you looking so glum?" asked the Wilbur ticket taker. "Your big boss is here tonight."

32

"That's why," I groaned. I explained how vital it was that I get the Colonel out of Boston right after the show. He suggested I call Fred Knight, at Northeast Airlines. He was in charge of public relations and might solve my problem.

I called Fred and explained my plight.

"How many are going back to New York?" he asked me.

"Four."

"Good. That gives me a reason to put on a special Show Plane. We do this on Saturday nights to accommodate the actors who want to go back to New York for the week end. Your four people give me enough to fill a plane," he said.

I rushed to the Northeast Airlines Office and changed the tickets for the special midnight flight. When I finally got back to the theatre, the usherettes had instructions not to seat anyone during a first act soliloquy. I managed to evade them and walked down the aisle in my squeaking, wet shoes, annoying the hushed audience as well as those on stage.

The Colonel was sitting on an aisle seat. He had saved a vacant seat for me between himself and his son. I squirmed into my seat. I told him I had the tickets for his plane, leaving at midnight. He patted me on the back, muttering: "That's my boy!"

As I sat down, the button on the sleeve of my coat got caught in the hairnet of a dowager sitting in front of me. The more I tugged the more it became snarled. The Colonel let out a roar of laughter.

The usherette ran down the aisle and flashed her light in the Colonel's face to keep him quiet. I finally untangled my sleeve from her hair.

"Take off your coat," the Colonel advised me.

"Where'll I put it?" I asked. He showed me how he had rolled his coat under his seat.

"I can't do that. It's my brother's coat," I said.

He emitted another raucous laugh. The usherette ran down

the aisle, again flashed a warning light in the Colonel's face.

Whether the Colonel regretted buying the play before he had seen it, I don't know. But Moger had bitten off his other five fingernails before we finally left the theatre.

At last we arrived at the airport.

"Who is that?" the Colonel asked me, pointing to a waiting passenger.

"That's Louis Calhern. He's appearing in Boston in *The Magnificent Yankee*," I informed him.

"Hya, Looey," he shouted to Mr. Calhern.

"Hello, Mr. Warner," said Calhern. "What are you doing in Boston?"

"Oh, I came to see my alma mater Lever Brothers play Procter and Gamble."

"What was the score?" asked Louis.

J.L. walked away without answering.

As we walked to the plane, I finally could joke again. "Too bad you didn't tell Calhern that the score between Lever Brothers and Procter and Gamble was: 'No soap!'"

Colonel Warner squinted at me and said sourly: "You should have quit when you were ahead and you could certainly use a-head, Art."

Ho—Hum!

SEEING IS BELIEVING!

I SAT IN THE limousine with lovely Jean Simmons and Mervyn LeRoy, en route to location in Marblehead for the filming of *Home Before Dark*.

As we passed by the State House in downtown Boston, Miss Simmons shouted: "Stop the car!"

The driver slammed on his brakes, she looked out of the window and asked:

"Do you see what I see?"

34

"What do you see?"

"Doesn't that sign in front of the State House say 'Hooker Entrance'?"

"What's wrong?"

" 'Hooker' means 'prostitute' in England. I'm surprised that staid Bostonians would be so blatant about advertising their whereabouts!"

I looked at the huge plaque on the State House wall and assured her that "Hooker Entrance" was in honor of Joseph Hooker, a Union General in the Civil War.

"HITCH" YOUR STAR TO A WAGON

"HITCH," as he is called by those who are fond of him, is known to millions as Alfred Hitchcock, the funny little man who enacts those zany commercials on his suspense-filled television programs. He is also one of the world's best motion picture directors.

It was during the filming of *I Confess* in Quebec, that I first met Hitch, his darling wife, Alma Reveille, a famous screenwriter, and daughter, Pat, a talented young actress.

"A critic once asked me why I don't make the kind of films I want to," he confided one day. "I would, but one word always creeps into the script: *Commercialism.*

"If I had my way, I'd innovate a unique way of showing the screen credits which usually bore the hell out of the audience. I'd like to see the credits shown in a toilet bowl. A hand will appear and flush away the credits. The next series of credits are shown. These are flushed down the toilet bowl, etc. etc.

"I also have a plot for a motion picture which I'd like to do sometime. A crazy galoot plants a time bomb under Yankee Stadium during a World Series. As thousands of people are watching the game, the audience is sitting on the edge of

35

their chairs, knowing that the bomb will go off and kill many innocent sports lovers. . . ."

"It sounds like a real thriller-diller," I commented. "Why don't you do it?"

"I would if I could think of a good ending!" he answered.

"Another theme that I would like to develop into a movie would be to show a big chase which ends up on Mt. Rushmore. I'd have the villain chase the hero up into President Abe Lincoln's nostril. But my problem is how do I get him out of there?"

"That's easy," I answered facetiously. "Let it take place in the winter. Lincoln's nose would be covered with ice. The sun starts to thaw out the ice and the hero slides out of the nostril pushing the villain to his doom below."

Ludicrous as this might have sounded, the basic theme became the plot of Hitch's successful movie, *North by Northwest*, starring Eva Marie Saint and Cary Grant. One of the highlights of the film was a chase on Mt. Rushmore. Hitch didn't use Lincoln's running nose episode, however, as I had suggested.

Hitch is a practical joker. He loves to do the bizarre. One afternoon, while in Boston on a personal appearance to publicize one of his many films, he asked me where the most fashionable women's store was located. I took him to a downtown specialty shop. No one recognized the cherub-like producer. He wasn't known as a TV personality then. We both waited until the elevator was filled with women and as the car started to ascend, Hitch began to talk so all could hear him:

"Wasn't that the goriest sight you ever saw, Art? When he jumped and landed against the building his head was bashed in so that you could see his entire brain structure. When he hit the pavement with a thud, six stories below, his eyeball rolled out of its socket and . . ."

36

The elevator stopped at the next floor. All of the women scampered toward the exit, including the elevator operator. We were left alone. Hitch broke out into loud laughter. We both stepped out of the elevator as the women peered at him from behind displays and mannequins.

"Alfred Hitchcock has become world famous for his methods of dealing with suspenseful situations, so it cannot come as a shock that he also has a reputation as a practical joker," observes H. Allen Smith in his hilarious and informing opus: *The Compleat Practical Joker.*

His gags are known on both sides of the Atlantic. He used to enjoy handcuffing people to things and leaving them there. He once had an old horse delivered to Sir Gerald du Maurier's dressing room at St. James' Theater. On another occasion he amused himself by sending four hundred smoked herring to a friend as a birthday gift.

A young actor once told me how he called on Mr. Hitchcock in his room at the St. Regis Hotel in New York. They left the room and got into the car and stood with their backs to two old ladies. Mr. Hitchcock and the actor had been talking about a motion picture but now the Hitchcock voice changed. A melodramatic tremor came into it, and he said:

"You know very well I had to shoot him. Had no choice. Don't really think I killed him. Aimed four shots at his leg. Left him in a pool of blood, lying on the floor. Suppose anybody heard the shots? You've got to stand by me on this. Have the taxi pick me up around the corner."

The moment this little monologue started the two old ladies began to stiffen. By the time the car reached the ground floor they were clearly in a state of horror. They were practically running when they left the car and zipped out of the hotel, heading for the street and safety, not even pausing to notify the management that foul murder had been committed on the premises and the murderer was making his get-away.

One of Hitchcock's victims in London tried to get back at him. He prepared a filthy concoction and poured it into a rare brandy bottle, replaced the seal, and presented the bottle to the director. Days passed and not a word from Mr. Hitchcock. Finally the man could stand the suspense no longer.

"That brandy I gave you," he said, "did you get a chance to sample it?"

"No," said Hitchcock, "I'm sorry to say I didn't. Didn't want to mention this to you, but my mother took sick. Doctor prescribed regular doses of brandy. We fed yours to her. I'm afraid it didn't help. Afraid she's going to die."

However, when newspapers reported an incident of someone throwing a lemon at Hitch as he headed up a delegation of Hollywood stars during a War Bond tour in Massachusetts, I wired him: "Congratulations. First time I ever heard of a lime-y being hit by a lemon."

For reply he sent me forty crates of lemons . . . express collect!

HYER(S) AND HYER(S)

THERE'S A GOOD STORY making the rounds about the drunk who accidentally walked into an open elevator shaft, fell twenty stories to the bottom, looked to the opening from whence he fell and shouted:

"I said 'Up'!"

Now this may or may not strike you as being funny. However, it appeared as a *true* story by co-star Martha Hyers, as a publicity yarn for *The Man From The Diners' Club* starring Danny Kaye. Here's how it came out:

You probably know that movies are never shot in the sequence the viewer sees in the final version. My introduction to Danny Kaye on the set of *The Man From The Diners' Club* was during the shooting of the scene which actually took place about the middle of the picture.

Danny's lean frame was crammed into a dumb-waiter. For this particular sequence, the dumb-waiter was supposed to rise rapidly from the basement of an apartment house to Danny's kitchen on the third floor. The scene had to be re-shot several times as the dumb-waiter stubbornly refused to go up quickly enough. Danny, his arms wrapped around his legs, his legs tucked tightly under his chin, was hunched quietly in the small metal car. Suddenly, as the dumb-waiter rose to about the second floor, something went wrong and it plummeted back down to the basement, thumping Danny against the bottom of the car with a resounding whack.

Director Frank Tashlin and the set technicians rushed over to the car to see if the star was hurt, but before they could reach him, Kaye peered out, looked at Tashlin and shrieked, "I said *up!*" That broke us up for a week.

Now, really. . . .

NEW FIELDS TO CONQUER

AMONG THE OLD TIMERS I met was the crimson, bulbous-nosed W. C. Fields, who has become a legend among movie-goers and stage votaries.

It is no secret that Fields frowned on the vast popularity of Charlie Chaplin, whom many consider the greatest panto-mimist in the world.

On one occasion Bill went to see one of Chaplin's more popular silent films. He couldn't watch him perform for more than a few minutes at a time without becoming resentful. After seeing the great silent comedian suffocate a 350-pound villain by pulling a street lamp around his neck, which caused the audience to scream with laughter, his only comment was, "The sonovabitch is a ballet dancer!"

However, he later wryly admitted: "He's the best ballet dancer that ever lived and if I get a chance I'll kill him with my bare hands!"

W.C. was the reason that a prominent cigarette manufacturer almost committed suicide. He insisted on refusing to delete a portion of his radio script in which he referred to his son as "Chester." He continually jabbed the sponsor by calling his radio scion by his whole name. Since the sponsor was "Camels," the name "Chester Fields" didn't add to his delight, especially since the cost of the radio show ran well into six figures.

I like to think that W.C. was equally as adept in pantomime as Chaplin. In many cases, I feel he was superior. The title of "The King of Comedy" should be bestowed upon him posthumously.

He played the perfect buffoon until the very end. Even in death he went out with a gag.

He died on the day that he pretended to detest . . . Christmas!

NO HONOR AMONG FIEFS

DOUGLAS FAIRBANKS, JR. has an English accent that you have to cut with a cricket stick. He was born in America, of course.

I was asked to meet him at the airport with the limousine which was to transport him to Lee, Massachusetts where his daughter was finishing school.

Now, I am not unlike Dave Susskind. I hate to be a manservant to a guy just because he speaks with an English accent or wears two-tone shoes.

So, I waited at the airport at BOAC until five A.M. when I was informed that due to a leaky water pipe or some such

God-awful excuse, the plane would be hours and hours late.

Finally, the dapper Mr. Fairbanks, Jr. arrived. He had to clear customs. We arranged for his photograph with one of the customs men so that his fans (I don't know how many he has now) would know he arrived in Boston at an unearthly hour.

He came with scads of baggage. At least twelve or more bags and suitcases. His chauffeur remained in the car. It could have been a Hertz car, at that. It never occurred to me to ask.

"How much do you think I ought to tip the skycap, Art, ole boy?" he asked me.

I looked over the baggage and said, "Oh, I'd say about ten dollars, Doug." (I get familiar with a celebrity very fast.)

"If you think that's enough for a movie star and one who is chairman of the board of Scripto pencils, it's okay with me," he remarked. Then after a brief pause, "you give it to him. I have only English currency, you know!"

Fairbanks, hell!

THE ORIGINAL "FIBBER" McGEE

HOLLYWOOD is a place where emotion triumphs over reason. It is a hamlet where "aping" one another is not confined to Tarzan alone. For example, one of the famous intersections of this movie capitol had a sign selling the wares of a used car sales agency: "Honest John, Used Car Dealer." A few days later, another billboard sign shouted the praises of a plumber, thusly: "Honest Carr, Used John Dealer."

When I received a call from Warner Bros. Studio and was told that Harry Warner, president of the company, wanted to talk to me, I quickly packed my bag, grabbed my hat, and took one step out of the door. This was the first time I had ever been called directly by the president.

"I see by the papers, Mr. Moger," began the aging head of the film company, "that you have a war hero by the name of McGee, from Worcester, Massachusetts. I want you to sign him up for us. I don't know what he can do, but we will make room for him no matter what he wants to do."

Mr. Warner had a reason for calling. He had lost his only son at the age of nineteen, when he was a student at Worcester Academy. After final exams, his son had developed a toothache and a dentist suggested treating the molar until he returned from a trip to Mexico. While in the Aztec country, young Warner's tooth kicked up and he went to a local dentist who extracted it. He developed an infection, spinal meningitis, and died.

Worcester Academy was endowed with a Warner Memorial Theatre by Harry M. Warner a few years later. So, it was only natural that Mr. Warner should want to continue honoring a Worcester citizen who had been acclaimed in the press from coast-to-coast as a maligned U. S. war hero, sentenced to hard labor and a dishonorable discharge for slapping a Nazi prisoner of war. After all, the Nazis had slapped around many of our boys, too, and we quickly forgave them.

I went to Worcester, bent on finding and signing up the great hero, Private Joseph V. McGee. I didn't know what he looked like. I didn't know where to look for him. However, Mr. Warner had issued a challenge.

I quizzed the Chief of Police. He knew the boy's father, a lineman with the telephone company. Both were members of the same World War I post. He summoned the father to the police station and I explained my mission.

"It's a good thing for Joe," said the Chief. "He's being wined and dined by the whole community. They are running Bond rallies for him and he has lots of money one day and is broke the next. Getting him away from these so-called friends is the best thing that can happen."

42

I called Gene Flynn, now director of Holy Cross College athletics, then in charge of public relations at Fort Devens, where McGee was stationed.

"Don't ask me about that guy," said Gene. "He's AWOL and too hot to handle. If you find him, tell him we'd like to have him come back. Don't urge him too much, though. The newspapers have been playing him up as the big hero of World War II and I don't want to be censured by telling them that he's been over the hill for nearly a week."

I went looking for the hero with his father. Where he was, nobody knew and Worcester is a big city. But, someone must have seen him.

Agreed that he would sign up with Warner Bros. I made a tour of the city with his father, trying to locate him. We finally spotted an open-collared GI coming out of a barbershop.

"There he is!" shouted his father.

We stopped our cab and invited young Joe to come in with us. He was a handsome youth, bedecked with more citations and ribbons than a Congressional Medal of Honor recipient.

I explained in detail that Warner Bros. wanted to put him under contract. If he wanted to drive a truck, we had the biggest and best trucks. If he wanted to act, we would make an actor out of him. There was nothing that he could ask for that we would not grant him. Salary was no object. "Just sign that you will go to work for Warner Bros.," I urged. His father told him to sign the release that I had prepared, there and then.

"How about the shrapnel on my brain?" he whispered to me.

"What shrapnel?" I asked.

"Sh-h-h," he mumbled so that his father could not hear. "I got wounded in the War and I need an operation. My father doesn't know about this."

43

"What are you worrying about, Joe?" I asked. "We have the best doctors in the world to take care of you." (I was thinking about Dr. Kildare and other "movie medics," including Dr. Ehrlich and his magic bullet, an old-time Edward G. Robinson epic.)

"Well, then," he added, "who'll take care of my wife? She's a Wren in the English Army. She's a nurse."

"I didn't know you were married," I replied, "but if you are, take her along, too."

"Well, I have to serve two more years in the Army," he added.

"Sign on the dotted line, Joe. This means that whenever you are ready, you have a job for life at one of the largest movie studios in the world."

Reluctantly, he signed, after we retired to the police station and the Chief urged him to "get out of town" as fast as he could for the good of the community as well as himself.

The ink hadn't dried on the release which made Private Joseph V. McGee the property of Warner Bros. Pictures, when I received a call at the Police Station. It was my wife, who had not heard from me for two days. I was too busy to check in at home, as I usually did. She had put in a call to the Worcester police to report me "missing." There I was with the Chief—himself!

Mr. Warner commended me in a wire for a fine job. My superiors were equally happy that the publicity department was so efficient.

A couple of days later, newspapers throughout the land announced in glaring headlines:

Court Martial Again Jails Nazi-Slapper
Worcester Private Admits Falsification

FORT DEVENS, July 10—Pvt. Joseph V. McGee of Worcester, 25-year-old Nazi slapper, who gathered much sympathy when imprisoned for mistreating prisoners, was sentenced to six months at hard labor today by a court martial after he pleaded guilty to three new charges.

McGee, who will also forfeit $35 a month of his $50 monthly pay, was charged with being absent without leave, with being drunk in uniform in a public place, and making with false oaths. The trial also brought out that McGee, many times described as a wounded, decorated hero, had never been decorated, never was in combat, and never had been wounded.

It was disclosed that in addition to not being entitled to wear the Purple Heart and the Silver Star, McGee admitted he had been convicted 13 times before by court martials on charges including AWOL, drunkenness, fighting, disrespect of a superior, illegally taking an Army half-track and mistreating prisoners.

The board deliberated only 10 minutes before returning a finding of guilty for McGee, who had gained nationwide attention and sympathy before being released from a two-year hard labor sentence with army re-instatement after the Nazi-slapping episode.

At the hearing military police officers testified they arrested McGee in Worcester June 30 when they found him drunk. They said he had no pass or furlough papers and that he resisted when they tried to place him in a police wagon.

Maj. Leon A. McCarthy, post judge advocate, testified that on June 5 he talked to McGee on the question of whether McGee was entitled to wear the Purple Heart and Silver Star.

The major said that McGee made a sworn statement at that time in which he said he was a member of B Co., 1st Battalion, 18th Infantry Regiment, 1st U.S. Infantry Division on Oct. 1, 1944, before the Siegfried Line; and that he and a Sgt. O'Rourke attempted to knock out a German pill box with grenades, during which action both were wounded. McGee, said the major, showed scars which he said were from the wounds.

Maj. McCarthy quoted McGee as saying that he was in a hospital in France and later in England as a result of the wounds, and that at the 96th General Hospital he was awarded both decorations.

The next day McGee told the major the same story, but

shortly afterward when confronted by Lt. Col. Sumner Elton, First Service Command judge advocate, with official excerpts from 1st Division records from Paris, McGee admitted that he had not been telling the truth, the court martial was told.

The records showed McGee had never been in the 1st Division, never was in combat or wounded, and had no right to wear either decoration.

Testifying in his own defense, McGee said his father was to have met him at the YD Club in Worcester on the night of June 25. He said he had a few drinks and didn't remember anything during the five-day period between June 25 and the time he was arrested.

"I don't know where I was; I guess I was drinking somewhere," McGee told the court martial officers.

He testified he had gone to school until he was 16 years of age; that he played "hooky" occasionally, and that he was sent to the Lyman School for truancy. He started serious drinking, he said, when he was in the Army in Panama, where rum was 65 cents a quart.

Maj. Charles A. Angelo, Army psychiatrist, testified he had examined McGee on June 4. He said he considered him "mentally old enough to make a statement" and that he could distinguish right from wrong.

Maj. Angelo said he rated McGee mentally as the equal of a person 11 years 6 months old by Army tests.

President of the five-man court was Maj. Frank Reeder of Newton Center. First Lieutenant Lee Epstein of New York was trial judge advocate, and Capt. Frank R. Bowler of Worcester, defense counsel.

McGee never did see the second wire I received from my west coast studio: "Forget McGee's agreement to come to work for us. We don't want him!" Signed: Harry H. Warner, President.

ME JAYNE—YOU STUPID!

THE FIRST TIME I ever laid eyes on Jayne Mansfield was one experience I'll never forget. I was eating at a local bistro when suddenly people dropped their knives and forks, dishes clattered, waiters and waitresses stood transfixed, everyone was mesmerized. Their gazes were directed towards the entrance of the eatery. There stood the behemothlike, Junoesque, blonde goddess of the sex symbol, Jayne Mansfield, dressed in a tight sweater. Her two mammoth mammary glands protruded around the corner until she made Jane Russel and Anita Ekberg look like adolescent boys.

She was appearing in a stage play, *Will Success Spoil Rock Hunter?* Warner Bros. had just completed a film, *Illegal,* starring Edward G. Robinson and Nina Foch. A pretty girl, dressed in a form-fitting sweater and blue jeans graced the billboards. This was an ingenue named Jayne Mansfield who had a brief role in the picture. Her personal appearance with the stage show gave me an excuse to hold a "press party" for the local critics to spearhead the film's opening.

As I walked over to her to introduce myself, the spell among the viewers was broken. She turned sideways and kissed me saying, "Oh, so you're the Warner Bros. press agent? Am I queer for press agents!"

She agreed to attend a private screening of *Illegal* and a luncheon for the drama editors and reporters the next day. We met at the Pilgrim Theater screening room. She sat next to me. As the house lights dimmed she reached out for my hand. The picture began and Miss Mansfield was enthralled with everyone, including her own brief appearance. Suddenly, in the movie, Ed Robinson gets his comeuppance. He is shot and lies on the floor writhing in pain and emitting sounds of "Yah, yah, yah." Nina Foch is bent over him tenderly.

I became aware that Jayne was sobbing loudly. Crocodilelike tears were running down my coat sleeve.

"Why are you crying?" I asked.

"Does he die?" she sobbed.

"Who?"

"Mr. Robinson," she sniffled.

"Of course not," I assured her. "He's making another film for us."

With this, she stopped crying, brushed aside a loose tear and began talking about a Philadelphia critic who called her "a Marilyn Monroe who could act."

Her screen biographies tell about her college curricula at Texas, California and other states. I asked one of her classmates about her mental prowess and scholastic aptitude at these various colleges.

"Oh, she went to these colleges, all right," he confirmed. "She didn't study anything," he added. "We studied *her!*"

She posed in the nude in art classes at these various schools of higher learning to earn enough money to support herself and an infant daughter.

Jayne was a *model* student!

A WEBB OF CIRCUMSTANCES

MANY PEOPLE ask me which of the movie stars are the easiest to get along with. It would be easier to single out those who are "the most miserable." One in particular was Jack Webb.

Not only was he the most temperamental (90 per cent temper and the rest . . .) but he was also the most recalcitrant. He also wins the title as the "homeliest" in my book.

We met while trying to publicize a film he made, *Pete Kelley's Blues*. He had just married one Dorothy Towne, a blonde, and was combining a junket with his honeymoon. This was Webb's second, after divorcing Julie London. He arrived via a private, chartered United Airlines plane, "The Mary Connors." Coming in from Canada it was mandatory that he land for customs clearance. However, he gave orders to the pilot to land on the regular commercial, domestic runway. Well, sir, all hell broke loose. The customs guards came running towards us. Mr. Webb, then the star of his own TV series, *Dragnet*, met the guards half way.

"I'm Jack Webb, the TV and movie star," he said.

"Oh, yes," replied one of the customs men. Obviously, the name didn't mean anything to him.

"You have landed on the wrong strip, sir. You will have to order the plane to come with us to customs for clearance."

"Wait just one minute, fellers. You don't realize who I am. Ask any of these guys," as he pointed a finger in the direction of six or seven flunkies and press agents who accompanied him on his coast-to-coast trip. "I'm Jack Webb, star of TV and movies."

"Look, mister, orders are orders. We have no jurisdiction over you here and you have no right to land here. So, please follow us to the further end of this strip."

Jack was carrying an attaché case. He turned to one of the apathetic custom officers and said:

"Confidentially, the bag I have here has a false bottom. It is full of heroin, but we won't tell anyone will we?"

The guard seized the bag. He went through every piece of paper in it. He also ordered all of the other bags to be opened. This went on for hours as a complete search was made of forty or more trunks, bags and manuscripts.

I often think that the officers did this on purpose. I know that they knew Webb was trying to be a wise guy. But, they had the last word!

We finally arrived hours late for a press interview at the Sheraton Plaza Hotel.

"Do you know if I can have a bill of sale notarized in the hotel?" Jack asked me.

I called Henry Francis, the assistant manager. He told me that he would be glad to notarize it.

"Will he charge me for it?" asked the big TV-movie star.

"Don't worry about it," I said. "At most it's fifty cents, if anything at all."

When Mrs. Webb was asked in an interview why she married Jack she said: "I'd rather marry a homely rich man than a handsome poor one." She must have withheld the published interview from Jack.

Everything we did seemed to be a crisis. Jack noticed some shoes that I was wearing. "They look like comfortable moccasins, Art. How much are they?"

"I think I paid fourteen dollars for them."

"Holy Jesus! I can get the same kind in L.A. for eight dollars."

"So why don't you?"

"Well, I thought you'd have some contacts here where I might get them even cheaper."

He sent his "valet,"—a Japanese student who joined the troupe in California to earn enough to go back to school—out for the moccasins. I gave the "valet" the address of Crystal's Shoe Store in downtown Boston. I called Harry Crystal and told him that it was permissible to give this fellow whatever he wanted and I'd be personally responsible. The "valet" returned with ten pairs of shoes. None fitted. Jack returned them all.

The next morning, Jack and his group were scheduled to fly to Pittsburgh at seven A.M. The night before, Boston was struck by its worst hurricane since 1938. Cellars were flooded. Lights went out. Boston was declared a disaster area. My own cellar had more than four feet of water. Furniture was floating around. The water seemed to come in from all sides of the house.

Seized by panic, I took an old Electrolux vacuum cleaner and thought that by reversing the action I could pump out water from the cellar onto the street. I asked my wife to help me, as both of us were immersed in water up to our waist

50

trying to plug the vacuum cleaner's electric cord into an outlet near the base of the heater. Luckily, we couldn't find it. If we had this could never have been written.

The next morning it continued to rain. I left my home wearing an old sweatshirt and a raincoat.

I arrived at the Sheraton Plaza Hotel at six thirty. I called Jack Webb from the house phone.

"I'll be right down," he said.

He soon came down, dressed in a light pair of pants and a cashmere sports coat. His wife joined him wearing a long, flowing, chiffon garden dress.

I thought to myself: "This character really believes his press clippings. Why doesn't he wear a trench-coat as he does on his TV series?" There was no one within five miles of the hotel who cared whether he existed or didn't.

I avoided him. He called me over.

"Hey, Art, how come there's nothing on the schedule about rain, today?"

Ordinarily, I'd take this as a gag. But I was sure he meant it.

NOT SO SAD SACK

CHARGING INTO the cavernous lobby of New England's biggest movie theater, the man with the big cigar gestured expansively at an abstract mosaic in ceramic tile. "Looka that, friend," he roared. "Know what it cost? Twelve big ones." (i.e., $12,000). Newly refurnished and reopened as the Music Hall, in July 1962, Boston's old, 4,250-seat Metropolitan Theater was undeniably cinemajestic. So, in his own way is its fifty-one-year-old boss—hefty (6 ft., 240 lbs.) Ben Sack.

Though television once seemed about to bankrupt movie-theater business, many cinemas are making money again by showing wide-screened, star-studded spectaculars for longer runs and at higher prices. Big Ben Sack, who operates five theaters in downtown Boston and is building a sixth, is a leading practitioner of the new formula. "He is the outstanding independent in the country," says one Hollywood booking executive.

Sack got into the theater business by accident. The son of immigrant Russian Jews, Sack owned four meat markets by the time he was nineteen, lost them at twenty when the depression hit. Turning to a truck driver's job with a scrapmetal firm owned by his in-laws, he soon wound up owning the company and by World War II was a happy "junkman" grossing fifteen million annually.

One evening in 1948 Sack returned to a gin rummy game he had just left to retrieve a forgotten gold pencil. At the table he fell into conversation with another player, ended up lending him $10,000 to renovate a movie house in Lowell, Massachusetts. The loan eventually expanded into a $200,000 investment in three theaters. When his partner decided to sell out, Sack suddenly found himself in the theater business. "What did I know about theaters?" he asks. "About as much as John Dillinger knew about being Pope."

Today, every theater owner in New England envies Ben Sack's brand of ignorance. Sack persuaded Hollywood to give him first-run rights in Boston to such films as *Bridge on the River Kwai* by offering a guarantee of $100,000, four times the top offer of his competitors. He pours out $600,000 a year to plug his shows by television, radio and massive five-column newspaper advertisements. "Looka that," he says scornfully of his rival's smaller ad. "It's like a death notice."

Sack staffs his theaters carefully and keeps the help honest by ringing in an occasional private detective disguised as a moviegoer to make sure the audience count is correct. He is insistent on cleanliness, will berate usherettes for not picking up paper from the aisles and scolds janitors when he finds

Alfred Hitchcock

Rita Hayworth

Elizabeth Taylor and Mike Todd

Top: Janis Paige
Center: Ruth Roman, Eva Six
Bottom: Alexis Smith, Doris Day

dust in the rest rooms. Sack likes to roam his lobbies, reminding women patrons that "this place is clean enough to bring your children to, right?" He has been known to step out of his $15,000, chauffeur-driven Cadillac in front of a Sack theater to hustle customers into the house like a sideshow barker.

Sack claims that his theaters are grossing $2,300,000 a year. He should do even better now that he has added the Music Hall, which cost him $600,000 to renovate. Along with movies, the big theater has booked the Bolshoi Ballet, the Metropolitan Opera and will be rented out to Boston firms for sales meetings. "What the hell do I care what they do in the morning?" says Sack. "I want it filled all day long."

LET GEORGE DO IT!

ONE OF MY favorite journalists is George Frazier. I have known him for more than twenty years. We are not bosom friends, not anything like that, but I admire him and his writings. He is an honest writer and has caused more commotion in staid Boston than Paul Revere did when he woke up a sleeping countryside shouting, "One if by land . . . two if by sea." If George had been around at the time, Paul Revere might have hired him to tell the citizens of Boston that trouble was about to descend upon them. Bostonians would have believed him and rallied to his cause.

Boston's most controversial writer, Frazier put adrenalin into the cups of coffee of thousands of sleepy-eyed readers of the *Boston Herald* with candid and unrestrained daily columns.

Time referred to Frazier as "Boston's uncommon scold." And had this to say about him:

"George Frazier is a man of muscular opinions. To him, Harry Belafonte is 'America's number one slave.' Mississippi's Governor Ross Barnett is a 'son of a bitch.' Roger Maris is a 'fink' and Mickey Mantle is an 'unfrocked fink.' In Frazier's considered judgment 'all hockey players are crazy,' all Texans are 'a little ridiculous,' and Brooks Brothers is 'like a giant class reunion.'

"Frazier is also constantly upset at life's imbalances. He is dispirited to find cars, not deer, at deer crossings; and when his thoughts drift to Howard Johnson's—a direction that Frazier's corpus rarely takes—they are wistful. 'If only Howard Johnson's would serve liverwurst sandwiches!' On the other hand, suitable equations gladden his heart. 'Tell the truth now—don't you think Pat Brown and California deserve each other?'

"These views, and others just as provocative, bloom in the barren soil of Boston, a city so unappreciative of common scolds that in the old days it put them in pillory. Many readers of the *Boston Herald*, where Frazier's column appears six times a week, write in to suggest that such punishment is much too good for the *Herald*'s uncommon scold. George Frazier, 52, is possibly the most roundly despised man in Boston . . . and the most widely read.

"That a man of Frazier's 'class'—to borrow one of his favorite words—should find harbour on the *Herald* is as unlikely as the discovery of Lucius Beebe's by-line in *Mad* magazine. Boston papers, the *Herald* included, rank among the dreariest in the land, a reputation enriched every year. One measure of Boston journalism is that the *Herald* hired Frazier in 1961 to replace four comic strips. No doubt the paper considered the exchange a compliment to their new man.

"What the *Herald* got was an undomesticated ego with the habit of erecting insults on the very borderline of libel. When Jack Ricciardi, Boston's commissioner of public works, faced the prospect of appearing as a witness before a U.S. Congressional committee (he was never summoned), all Frazier could talk about was Ricciardi's curly hair. 'My own

54

view,' wrote Frazier, 'is that if U.S. Representative John Blatnik has any feeling for beauty, he will first compliment Mr. Ricciardi on his barber. Then, if he has any investigative zeal, he will inquire how many strokes with the brush Mr. Ricciardi gives those dazzling locks each night.' Enraged, Ricciardi consulted his lawyer, who advised: 'All he's said is that you have a nice head of hair. You can't sue for that, my friend.'

"Frazier's rhetorical flights carry readers past such disquieting polysyllables as 'crepuscular,' 'demetry' and 'blevins.' The last, as hundreds of Bostonians discovered after vainly combing the dictionary, is no word at all, but a typographical error. Frazier meant Bruins, the name of the city's ice hockey team. The point is not that some *Herald* hand faltered, but that Frazier's followers faithfully went on a blevins hunt." (Including Yrs. Tly.)

"The son of a West Roxbury, Mass., fire inspector, Harvard man ('33), George Frazier has spent most of his life as a freelance writer and a full-time embellisher of his self-anointed role of an eccentric. When the mood hits him, he drives 464 miles to Buffalo, where the Charter House Motel serves a salad dressing to his taste. He wears $265 suits, brings his own hot dogs to baseball games, and snoots the common man. 'Can it seriously be argued,' he asked, after observing the deportment of a hockey crowd, 'that these ignorant, ill-clad, ill-spoken hooligans—common men all—are the equals of the civilized products of Groton?' All this, Frazier hopes, qualifies him as something of a snob. It is a badge he wears proudly, like the Legion of Honor.

"Frazier's hauteur is not confined to Boston Common. During a visit to New York, he found the new American Hotel 'more awful than anyone can imagine,' and densely inhabited by 'all the brassy blondes whom you seem to remember from Miami, all the sharp-featured characters in their wrap-around polo coats.' Turning away disdainfully, he trained his eye on the city's newspaper strike, found an unexplored facet: the special travail of Manhattan's paper-trained dogs. 'It strikes you as so strange,' Frazier wrote, 'to hear one woman complain, "I just don't know what I'm to do about my dog—my poor little Curt. He was so used to the *Times* that he simply won't have anything to do with any other paper." It seems so certifiable to hear somebody say something like that, and yet, when you stop to think about it a minute—why, what could make such sense?' "

Only George Frazier.

SO YOU WANT TO BE A MOVIE STAR?

SOMEONE ONCE MUSED: "The best laid plans of mice and men . . ." I have never seen a mouse lay a plan. Another mouse, maybe!

Press agentry and publicity thrive on circumstance. If you are at the right place at the right time you may come up with a lucky news "plant" or a good picture which may net valuable free space. A few months ago I was on tour with John Ashley, the handsome, teen-age star of many TV series and, more recently, the film *Beach Party*.

Mr. Ashley had been sent to New England to publicize his film, one of the season's all-time high attendance-getters.

One night, after a hectic session at a drive-in theater in Hyannis, Massachusetts, I tried to rescue John from the very rough plaudits of his teen-age audience.

"Salinger is on the phone, John," I told him grinning.

"Pierre Salinger?" asked one of the kids nearby, waiting for her third autograph.

"Man, you are the craziest," replied Ashley as I whisked him away into the pizza-making room of the Hyannis Drive-

In Theater. "That was a great exit-line if I ever heard one."

"Exit, shmexit," I answered, "let's get something to eat. I've made reservations at the Yachtsman's Club."

We posed for more pictures with the manager and his bosses who were all smiles—business was never better. As a gimmick we had chosen Hyannis as the typical "Teen Town, U.S.A." Why? Well, it seemed that fifty-one Junior Chamber of Commerces had vied for this honor. Hyannis was chosen because its teen-agers had the highest scholastic standing and lowest rate of juvenile delinquency. (When I told this to a newspaper editor, Milt Cole of the *Cape Cod Standard Times,* he said: "You must mean in the winter!"

John finished crowning "Mr. and Miss Teen Town, U.S.A." and gave them their prizes.

Exhausted we finally got to our table at the club. We had to order quickly. The chef was going home. We nursed a drink while we waited. A trio was making music on a stage, about fifty feet from our table. The combo consisted of a fellow in a bright red silk jacket playing the piano with his head cocked to one side, a bass fiddler who was plunking out a note here and there, and a drummer, a bleached blonde with a tight fitting white dress and a microphone around her neck.

"Let's give a big hand to Hollywood's newest star of *Beach Party,*" the drummer shouted through her mike. "Everybody meet John Ashley. With a little encouragement he'll sing for us."

I pushed John into the limelight and he walked towards the bandstand.

He sang *Old Cape Cod* and returned to the table.

"Do you know somethin', Art," he muttered. "That guy in the red jacket is the spitting-image of Pierre Salinger."

We both laughed at the inanity of the implausible situation.

The man in the red jacket finished playing. He came towards our table. He extended his hand to John.

"You sing very well. I wish you the best of continued success in whatever you do, John."

"Thank you, sir," said Ashley. "Did anyone ever tell you that you are a ringer for Pierre Salinger?"

"I ought to be," said the stranger. "I *am* Pierre Salinger!"

The next morning the story of Ashley and Moger recognizing Salinger was chronicled by Louella Parsons. Good publicity is often just luck!

PART TWO

who the hell is moger, anyway?

> *Half the world is squirrels;*
> *the other half is nuts!*
> —My brother Nate

HELLO, JOE . . . WHADDYA KNOW?

JOSEPH E. LEVINE has been publicly acclaimed as a combination of P. T. Barnum, Mike Todd, Harry Reichenbach with a slight smattering of Irving Thalberg. ("What happened to God?" mused one exhibitor.) Whatever his comparison, he's just plain Joe to those who knew him "when." Joe's first venture as a producer was with Commander Richard Evelyn Byrd of the fashionable Brimmer Street, Boston. It was called: *Discovery*, a story of the handsome Commander's visit to the North Pole.

Joe's second picture was a compilation of old film humor patched together into a feature film titled: *Gaslight Follies*. (It was.)

Today, the name Joseph E. Levine conjures motion picture epics in the best traditions of a Cecil B. DeMille or Darryl F. Zanuck. Although many enviable producers will tell you, in no uncertain terms, that Joe isn't in the same league as these tycoons, you will have to admit that Big Joe (a moniker I gave him because he is short and pudgy) has put the "show" back into showmanship. One day he's in his Sutton Place apartment, with his pretty wife, Rosalie, a former singer with Rudy Vallee's orchestra in the '30's, then he's off to supervise the production of films in Hollywood, Italy, Africa or wherever his multiple crews may be working.

He once told me: "You can't win with scared money. When you spend it, don't think of it as money. If you do, you're dead." Maybe that's why his press parties are as lavish as a Roman orgy . . . with all the trimmings.

A self-admitted former Boston dress salesman, Joe is one of the financial geniuses of an ailing motion picture business.

He has built up a number of relatively obscure (and not so good, from the point of view of critics) foreign films into staggering smash hits at the American box offices.

He bought the Italian-made *Hercules* for $125,000 and invested that much again in adding new sound effects and attractive titles. He then borrowed one million dollars from the First National Bank of Boston to show to motion picture exhibitors that he was spending that much for exploitation. The exhibitors were so impressed with Joe's showmanship and the sight of the million dollars, which was watched over by armed guards (supplied by the bank to protect its investment) that it was booked into more than seven hundred theaters at one time. This is now known as "a Joe Levine saturation campaign." By the time the reviews came out (and they were universally bad) the monies had poured into the coffers of the box office and Joe "had arrived." (He also made a star out of a muscle-man named Steve Reeves.)

"Maybe it didn't satisfy the critics, but the eighty per cent of the people who go to the movies loved it. It grossed over fifteen million dollars . . . more than eighteen million people saw it," adds Joe. (Since then, *Hercules* has appeared on television and countless millions more have seen it. How much Levine has realized from its sale is a secret.)

He then launched a sequel, *Hercules Unchained,* which also benefited by his innate sense of exploitation. He is a firm believer of the truism: "There has never been a motion picture made which didn't have to be sold." He makes them and sells them.

Admitting that his personal hero is P. T. Barnum, Joe operates on the theory that it is better to spend yourself rich than save yourself into bankruptcy.

"Many good pictures come out of Hollywood and fail because nobody knows about them. They aren't exploited properly," says Joe.

"Pictures are a circus business and you-gotta use circus techniques. If you don't advertise today, you don't sell—and I don't care what your picture is.

"You can last in business as long as you give the public what they want . . . and don't cheat them."

He has proven this. Such stars as Bette Davis, Sophia Loren, Alan Ladd (who made his comeback in *The Carpetbaggers,* in the choice role of Nevada Smith), Marcel Mastrianno, Elizabeth Ashley (a star as a result of her role in *The Carpetbaggers* admit that Big Joe knows what it is all about.

His rise is more incredible than Horatio Alger's. Joe was one of a family of thirteen children. He shined shoes and sold newspapers as a boy. He quit school at fourteen; once owned a chain of dress shops; had been a regional picture distributor for twenty-five years.

His program of exploitation has been so successful over the past eight years that canny foreign producers now have jacked up the price of their films, making it impossible to do now what Joe started.

Poor no more, Levine has arranged to co-produce abroad more of the turgid, colorful spectacle movies he favors. It is rumored that Paramount Pictures will become a fifty-fifty partner with Joe's Embassy Films. In some circles it is rumored that Joe will take over Paramount Pictures. (Shades of Cecil B. DeMille!)

Whenever he is confronted by bankers and business associates about his big budgetary splurges, the gregarious showman dismisses their objections with a genial wave.

"You can't win with scared money," he reminds them.

Earl Wilson calls him, "Quiet Joe, the wild bull of the movie producers." He likes to talk about the time that Joe gave three parties in three cities in three nights for Sophia Loren at the cost of $50,000. Joe modestly admits, "I'm no Perle Mesta."

Joe has a great sense of humor, too. When confronted with the fact that he chases around the world arranging pictures with Anita Ekberg, Romy Schneider, Claudia Cardinale and Bridgette Bardot, someone remarked:

"Your pictures are predominantly sexy."

"Some of my best friends are predominantly sexy," said Joe.

Joe is the kind of a guy who likes to take the orchestra home with him at 4 A.M., who burns $100 bills in front of you (some say it is a magic trick, others say Joe likes to show off that money doesn't mean that much to him). He seldom brags about his success but friends will tell you that he holds a Broadway record of having eight first-run movies on the Great White Way at the same time.

It's par for the course, for Levine to get films rolling in Hong Kong, Zululand, Formosa, in Italy, Russia and oh, yes, Hollywood.

The Italian government has honored him for making Italy one of the foremost film capitals in the world.

"I guess in Italy they won't like me making a picture in Hollywood," comments Joe. "They'll call me a 'run-away producer.' " (A "run-away producer" is a term applied to those who make films abroad to avoid taxes, use cheaper help, and sundry other reasons).

His comptroller interrupted our conversation by informing Joe that one of his films would gross $10,000,000.

Joe remarked, "Good. We can use that for petty cash."

I remember being with Joe in his Boston office. It was raining hard outside.

"Look, I just got a personal note for sixty-six thousand dollars. I haven't got sixty-six cents. Hang around. I'm gonna call my banker."

He dialed a number. He asked for a Mr. ———.

"Hi, this is Joe Levine. I got your note today. I have to go back to Hollywood this evening. I can't leave the office. Will you come up to see me? Okay, I'll wait for you."

Hanging up the phone he said to me, "Just wait until this bastard comes up here. You'll see the great Levine in action."

About fifteen minutes later, Mr. ——— arrived. I was introduced to him. I recognized him as the top echelon at one of Boston's leading banks, specializing in loans to movie producers.

"How's everything, Joe?" asked the banker.

"Great," answered Joe. "You know, I think I'm gonna need about three mill more for the picture I'm making."

"Hm," muttered the banker. "I think we can arrange that, Joe."

Nothing was said about the $66,000 personal note that Joe owed. I'm sure it was paid back out of the "three mill" that Joe finally received. Joe nodded to me and I left.

Maybe the best accolade paid to Joe's acumen and success, was one which I overheard one of his enviable "friends" utter at a recent luncheon hosted by Big Joe.

"You gotta give him credit. He's got balls!"

I'm sure he has.

BOOKING A TITLE

WHATEVER HAPPENED to those old-fashioned book titles which told you at a glance what the stories were all about? Remember the good old days when you could walk up to a bookshelf and pick out a volume with a self-explanatory title such as: *The Bobbsy Twins Go On Vacation* or *Frank Merriwell at Yale?*

The title was self-revealing. You knew immediately what to expect when you plunked down a couple of bucks for something to read. Today a book title *Batter Up* may sound like a compilation of World Series statistics, but is actually a treatise on how to make pancakes. Polly Adler's book, *A House Is Not A Home*, might be re-titled, *A Tart Is Not A Pastry*.

This book was originally called *Name Dropper*. Some of the short anecdotes were heard on Jack Paar's *Tonight* show. Jack told me that the contents of the book were great but that the title was bad. I thought otherwise. He enlightened me that a "name dropper" is a fraud, a phoney who drops a name here and there to recapture the attention of the listeners. "Come up with a title like Jack Douglas does."

He has some weird ones: *My Brother Was An Only Child* and *Never Trust A Naked Bus Driver*.

I returned with the title: *Some Of My Best Friends Are People*. He liked it. I hope you do, too. Since millions now judge a book by its cover, my friends are adding their title suggestions.

Jack McMahon likes: *Washington A.C. or D.C.?* "It should sell like hot-cakes among the electrical workers," he admits.

Dick Gregory, the famous Negro comedian says: "There doesn't seem to be any racial problem in this country. Everyone I talk to says: 'Some of my best friends are colored!'

"Now I know that isn't true, because there aren't that many colored people to go around!"

Joe E. Lewis suggested a title. *Up Your Bracket,* with a theme for those who want to increase their incomes and not their income taxes.

CBS's Bob Frank likes *TV Is Radio With Eyestrain.*

Mel Wintman, an executive with many bowling centers says: "Call it *You Can Hear A Pin Drop.*" A clothier, Jack Lane, wants *Don't Let It Go to Waist.* My insurance broker brother-in-law, Jess Rosen, likes: *You Can Bet Your Life.* My druggists, Willie and Ben, (Schwartz and Baker, that is) like: *Don't Be A Dope.*

However, my wife has the best suggestion of them all:

"Call it *A Best-Seller.* Doesn't every author want to have 'a best-seller'?"

I think she has something there.

WHAT'S IN A NAME?

ONE AFTERNOON the telephone at my parents' home rang. My dad answered it. The voice on the other end began:

"My name is seaman first class, Charlton Worthington Moger III. I am attached to a destroyer in the Boston shipyard. My home is in Monomonee Falls, Wisconsin. Whenever I come to a port I run through the telephone book to see if there are any other Mogers. My family is more than ten generation Mogers. I wonder if you are one of my kinfolk?"

My father hesitated for a brief moment, then, yelled:

"Oy . . . have you got the wrong number!"

Now the name "Moger" is uncommon. In Yiddish it means, "skinny" or "thin." I suppose, many years ago, my family was on the thin side. You can't prove it by me, although my dad didn't vary a pound in fifty years . . . and he was thin.

When my son, Stan, attended Colby College, in Waterville, Maine, his roommate was a fellow named Clint Moger, pronounced "Mojer." (We pronounce it "Moger" with a *hard* "g.") Coincidence? It must be, for this is the first time we ran across a living being with the same name as ours, yet, not related. I did see, once, a clipping about a blind sea captain from Buffalo whose name was Gil Moger. I wrote to him, but he never answered. Then there was Seth Moger, Dartmouth's great football star, also no relation!

You can imagine my surprise when I came across a passage in H. Allen Smith's *Let The Crabgrass Grow*, wherein he mentioned a "Moger Avenue." My dad told me that such a thoroughfare existed somewhere in upstate New York, but he didn't know where. It's in Mount Kisco.

I wrote to Mr. Smith, who answered:

"Moger Avenue now has a new refurbished saloon, very handsome and stylish, replacing a gin-mill where in previous years they were proud of their clientele's hardiness and never-washed beer glasses."

Another of Mount Kisco's stalwart citizens is Bennett Cerf. His knowledge of the derivation of the name Moger Avenue is also limited. He wrote me: "I am sorry to say that I can add nothing to your stock of information on the name of Moger. I've walked up and down Moger Avenue in Mount Kisco, of course, on many occasions, but don't know to this moment why it is called Moger Avenue. Our place in Mount Kisco is on *Orchard* Road; I've never heard of *Mr. Orchard* either!"

Maybe one of my kinfolk slipped into Mount Kisco one foggy night, set up a street sign and disappeared. I doubt it. But, it's mighty thrilling to walk along a street and point with pride to a sign overhead which bears your name, *Moger Avenue!* Yessir, it's a proud feeling. I must do it sometime.

MY FIRST ASSIGNMENT

HARRY SIMARD was a little photographer, with an ill-fitting toupee. He was a member of the Hearst newspapers for years. He almost killed the late William Randolph Hearst when he used a flash powder contraption which nearly blew up the great newspaper publisher and himself. In the old days they used dynamite to supply the "flash" for proper artificial light. He had added too much powder. This led to the abolishment of "powder" for flash pictures.

I met Harry when he covered assignments for me when I served as the news correspondent for the *Boston American* as an undergraduate at Boston University.

I'll never forget Harry's nonchalant attitude. It was during a murder on Joy Street, Boston. I accompanied Herbie Alpert, then a cub reporter and now a successful hotel tycoon.

We entered a dirty room and the body of the victim was lying on the floor. In addition to rifling the desks of the murdered man (this was par for a good newspaperman, in those halcyon days of the "scoop") we stole photographs of the deceased, his family and relatives.

"Let me take a picture of him lying on the floor," said Harry.

"His eyes are closed," I remarked.

"Oh, that's easily fixed," Harry said. He took out two common pins from the lapel of his suit. Kneeling down he lifted up the eyelids of the victim and pierced the pins into the skin above the eyelids.

This was my first assignment. It was damn near my last!

WHAT'S THE ANSWER?

AMONG THE MANY prolific qualifications and monikers I have tried to live down is: "The youngest contest editor in the world." An entire nation was made cognizant of this fact when Fred Allen introduced me to a coast-to-coast audience, the same night as the return match between boxing behemoths, Joe Louis and Max Schmeling. *Town Hall Tonight* allotted me eleven minutes of choice script with the master of *ad libs*, extolling the virtues of contests and contestants. At that time I was Contest-Puzzle Editor of the *Boston American*, the youngest and most underpaid in the whole universe.

As a result of the program, the following article appeared in *The Quill*, official publication of Sigma Delta Chi, honorary national journalism fraternity. It expressed my views about contests, at that time. "If youse guys and gals covering beats, interviewing big shots, little shots, blanks and duds thinks you have troubles, just listen to this!

"To begin with, I am a Puzzle Editor and have been for a long time. You can quote me as saying, without reservation, that the greatest collection of screwballs in the world makes contests its happy hunting ground . . . but don't get me wrong . . . I love contests!"

Various degrees of intelligence, of course, are represented in newspaper contests. The contestants include a large number of teachers, lawyers, business men, doctors, college professors and other professional men along with the scores whose collective I.Q. is considerably lower.

The life of a Contest Editor would indeed be a happy one if his troubles and anxieties ceased with the termination of a contest. Mrs. Sadie Zulch storms into the office, usually accompanied by meek Mr. Zulch, who stands in the corner chewing a toothpick. Mrs. Zulch is indignant because she didn't win the first prize of $5000. As a mater of fact, she's sore because she didn't win anything. Why?

After finding her entry, it was discovered that she misspelled four names; didn't know the identifications of six others; and neglected to write a letter, required of all contestants.

Is she pacified when her errors are shown to her? Does she acknowledge the misspelled names? No, sir!

She looks at the Contest Editor and barks brusquely:

"It's in the bag! And what's more, I'll write to the President about this!"

Slightly exaggerated? You wouldn't believe half of the problems which confront the puzzle editor—problems which seem unanswerable!

There was the WPA worker who burst into my office looking for the contest guy. "What's the idea of me not gettin' no prize?" he growled.

I asked him why he thought he was entitled to one. He said he had checked his list of solutions with those we had published the previous day in our newspaper, and that he had a one hundred per cent score. Naturally, he thought he was entitled to a prize and he wouldn't leave the office until given a satisfactory explanation.

Well, to make a long story short and boring, we dug up his entry, and when I say dug up, I mean it literally. It's no easy task looking through thousands of entries in search of one which may be in any of a hundred different files. Upon the discovery of his entry, it was found that he had misspelled such names as Katharine Hepburn, spelling her first name Katherine; Mabel Todd as Mable; Sidney Blackmer as Sydney; etc.

The entrant blinked a little and remarked:

"Well, I got the right idea, ain't I?"

But Contest Editors don't pay off for ideas. It's their job to think them up and it's the public's task to solve them.

In launching a contest, a great deal of expense and work is involved, ofttimes with questionable results.

In one of our contests dealing with movie stars' identifications, a chain of downtown theaters cooperated with us in exhibiting a trailer, announcing the details of the contest, the number of prizes, the amount of awards, etc.

One of the first trailers was sent to a downtown movie house which was showing a picture called *Nothing Sacred.* A sequence depicted Charles Winninger, as a small-town doctor berating Frederic March, a newspaper reporter.

The gist of the conversation was something like this:

"Oh, so you're a newspaper reporter, are you? Well, let me tell you something. I once entered a newspaper contest sponsored by your newspaper and do you know what? It dealt with an essay on who the six greatest statesmen were. I had a gem of a letter, but did I win any of the prizes totaling ten thousand dollars? No, sir! Did I win a second prize? No! Did I win even a dollar? No! I'll tell you who won the big prize, the managing editor's mother-in-law!"

The audience was convulsed with laughter.

A few minutes before this hilarious speech, our announcement trailer had blazoned across the huge screen, explaining "a bigger and better contest with $10,000 in cash prizes!"

Why this contest was one of the most successful ever run by the newspaper, I don't know. But, for a few moments, the Contest Editor was seriously thinking of selling gardenias outside of the *Boston American* building.

Have you ever heard of contest solutions being received in a newspaper office *before* a contest began?

An advertisement appeared in the *Boston Daily Record* a few days prior to the actual publication of puzzle pictures in a movie contest. The puzzles were to appear every weekday in the *Boston American*. They consisted of pictures containing scrambled names of movie stars. A series of forty-nine was to be printed. When properly arranged these scrambled letters spelled the names of popular movie stars.

The advertisement, prepared by the promotion department, was embellished with four stars, which were drawn merely for decorative purposes. It told readers to watch the *Boston American* for a big $10,000 cash prize movie contest called: "Name the Movie Stars."

The day after the ad appeared, I received a letter from Chicopee Falls. It read:

"Enclosed find my solution to your contest. I have named the four stars. They are: First Star, North Star; Second Star, South Star; Third Star, West Star; Fourth Star, East Star. Please send me the first prize $5000. I need the money."

Do you wonder that Contest Editors need a sense of humor?

MAMA'S BOY

I WAS CALLED A "mama's boy."

If a "mama's boy" meant coveting my mother and father; obeying them so that I brought home my week's salary and taking a meagre allowance (they banked the rest for me); not staying out too late when I went on a date (many is the time they called me at 10:30 P.M. and told me to come home, much to the chagrin of my "date"); being righteous, friendly to my fellowman and instilled with religion; then I was truly a "mama's boy."

Did it do me any harm? I don't know. It reminds me of the story of the M.C. who introduced a world famous maestro to an overflowing audience at an auditorium. No sooner had the aged maestro lifted his baton when he suddenly dropped dead.

The M.C. stepped in front of the lowered curtain and said:

"As you have just witnessed, the maestro, whom we brought here at great expense has suffered a fatal heart attack. He is dead!

With that a voice from the balcony shouted: "Give him an enema!"

Ignoring this gross statement the M.C. went on further:

"We shall refund your monies at the box office and deeply regret . . ."

"I said give him an enema!" continued the voice from the balcony.

"To you in the balcony, making those remarks, may I add that this man is dead . . . and an enema won't do him any good," concluded the M.C.

"I know," shouted back the balcony visitor, "it won't do him any HARM either!"

MY SON—THE JOKE-MAKER

"COME FLY BACK WITH ME," said Danny Kaye. It was an evening in November. My son, Stan, was being Bar Mitzvahed.

"Not a chance," I said. "I'm not going with you in your plane (the publisher of the *Toronto Mail* had loaned it to Danny) and find out that we didn't get there on time. I'm taking a train tonight."

"I would like to attend your son's Bar Mitzvah," Danny said seriously. "I haven't played a 'Bar Mitzvah' in years."

I arrived just in time at Temple Beth Zion. My son, Stanley, was good. After the service we adjourned across the street for dinner.

While we were eating I was called to the door. Somebody was asking for me.

It was Danny Kaye with Eddie Dukoff.

"I won't enter unless someone gives me a fountain pen,"

72

Danny laughed. It was customary to give pens as gifts at these affairs.

My nephew, Richard Rosen, rose to the occasion and gave Danny a pen from his pocket.

Stanley stood up and addressed the crowd:

"I want you to know that I have written a speech, myself. This is without the help of my parents or the Rabbi."

"Boy, I hate to think what the kid will say," Danny whispered.

"If it's my kid be prepared for anything," I replied.

"I just want you all to know that I hope I grow up to be a good Jew like Maxie Rosenbloom."

Stanley sat down. That was the end of his speech.

Danny ran up to him, extended his hand and said:

"That's the first time I ever had anyone top me! You were great!"

POLITICIANS ARE A STRANGE BREED

WORKING FOR POLITICIANS is no easy chore. Managers, co-managers, advisors and other members of the inner sanctum are on hand to give their unbiased opinions. Such was the case when I prepared the art work for one of the first political cartoon-type books, used in a state-wide political campaign.

"You'll have to get the approval of Senator Henry Cabot Lodge, Jr. as well as all of the other candidates before we can finalize anything," said Charley Nichols, the director of the Massachusetts Republican State Committee. "Lodge is the kingpin. If he says 'Okay' you're in."

I sought out Senator Lodge and his aide, Maxwell Rabb, who later became Secretary to the Cabinet under President Eisenhower.

"The drawing is just fine," he said.

I then went to Clarence Barnes, who was running for re-election as Attorney General, Albert Leman, who had been my "boss" when he was Sunday Editor of the *Boston Post,* was the official "advisor" to the Massachusetts Republican Party with an office in the State House. All media publicity had to clear through him.

Since I was convinced that he would not like the general idea because it had come from outside the organization, I went to him with trepidation. I showed him the drawing of Clarence Barnes. Hon. George Rowell, the first Assistant Attorney General, liked my work and this drawing in particular.

"Let's go into the General and show him the drawing," said George. Leman followed behind us. He wasn't a man of too many words as a rule. He spoke very fast and usually stuttered when he became excited. He seemed to be in a stage of constant excitement.

"Come in, boys," said Clare, as he was commonly called by those who were close to him.

"Here's a drawing that Moger did for the comic-book the Committee is planning," said George. "How do you like it?"

Leman grabbed the drawing and threw it, face up, on the floor. He jumped up on a sofa and asked Barnes to do likewise. As they both stood on the sofa, Leman fashioned his fingers in the shape of a jeweler's eyeglass and held it close to his right eye closing his left eye at the same time. He told Barnes to do the same. They both stood looking at the drawing on the floor below, squinting through one eye.

"Whatinhell am I supposed to see?" asked the Attorney General.

"I dunno," replied Leman. "I've been doing this for the last thirty years as a newspaper editor. Some artist told me that you see something clearer this way. What do you think, Clare?" he asked.

I held my breath. I waited for the Attorney General to speak!

"I think it's a pisser!" commented the General.

ONCLE ITZEL

HIS NAME was Isaac Reyn, pronounced "Ryan." Somehow or other we always called him "Uncle Itzel." He was my mother's cousin, actually. Since he was her nearest of kin, we adopted him as our Uncle. Pop called him "Oncle."

As an innkeeper, he was proficient in interpreting a grocery slip or a check number as an omen for the "numbers' pool." He usually spent between $5.00 and $10.00 daily with the local bookie. Hardly a day went by but Oncle Itzel made a "hit."

I recall one day he came to our home and showed us thousands of dollars. It seems that a customer had a dream and saw the numbers 1-9-7-2. Oncle played the four numbers and won almost $6,000.

He never played cards or horses. "Numbers" was his game.

When things got slow Oncle Itzel went into semi-retirement. He asked me to get him a job. (He had a bundle stashed away.)

I called my good friend Harry Wasserman, district manager of many theaters in the film district. Harry was very kind and understanding. He hired Mr. Reyn as a doorman for the Mayflower Theater in downtown Boston. Oncle Itzel was a good choice. The doorman's uniform fit him with little or no alterations. This, I am sure, influenced Harry in hiring him for the job.

Oncle held the record of having filled up a theater with one ticket stub. He was substituting for the regular ticket taker. A fleet of sailors came into town. They all headed for the Mayflower Theater where a popular motion picture was playing. The entire crew of sailors walked into the theater, each pointing to the one in back of him, when Oncle asked for their tickets.

The last sailor gave Oncle a ticket—just ONE! Itzel scratched his head and said: "So it's a mitzvah! A sailor is a sailor. So what's the difference? One ticket or a hundred?"

He met his demise when one of the theater owners, Marty Mullin (owner of one half of the Mullin and Pinanski chain) passed by and heard Oncle shout to hundreds of passers-by on busy Washington Street:

"Best seats in the *balcon!* Best seats in the *balcon!* See President Roosevelt in his best role wid James Cagney. Best seats in the *balcon!*"

Oncle never could tell when the newsreel ended and the feature film started. To him, FDR in the newsreels was a companion to Jimmy Cagney in a gangster role in the feature which followed.

Mullin turned livid with rage. He ordered Harry to fire *that* doorman. Harry did, but Oncle forgot to turn in the doorman's uniform. He wore it on Sundays to gain admittance into leading theaters and auditoriums. After all, who questions a doorman?

PUT HEARST IN THE DRIVER'S SEAT

"THEY DON'T MAKE newspapermen the way they made Walter Howey," reflects George P. Hollingbery, former member of the Hearst advertising staff in Chicago.

Walter Howey is the composite of all the newspaper editors you see in the movies. He is best portrayed in *The Front Page* as "Walter Burns," written by Ben Hecht-Charles MacArthur, two reporters who worked for him. If there was no story about thievery, bribery, rape, mayhem, kidnapping or brutality, Howey knew how to make them happen. He was a newspaperman, first and foremost. The wire services and pools of information have made the "scoop" or "exclusive story" a thing of the past. Reporters and editors like Howey are something of the past, too.

Probably nothing caused Howey more concern than missing out on a sensational headline. Dorfman recalls the "Howey legend," vividly. It concerns the assignment of two writers and a photographer to sit with a woman whose spouse was sentenced to hang for a dastardly crime he had committed. When word came of the man's death, the distraught widow tried to take her own life by leaping out of a window.

"I stopped her, boss!" one of Howey's reporters happily reported to him on the telephone.

"You damned fool!" he cried. "Why didn't you let her jump? We'd have had a scoop, you blundering idiot!" (I am sure he used other epithets which were much stronger!)

Another of Howey's obsessions was to get a corpse of a man who had been put to death by the state and have a doctor revive him. He then wanted to hire a person, not unlike Lazarus to write his experiences for Howey's newspaper. (Lazarus, according to the Bible, was a brother of Mary and Martha, whom Jesus raised from the dead.)

Incredible and gruesome as it may sound, Howey had tried to obtain a murderer's body several times in Chicago. With all of his contacts, personal and political, he never realized his secret ambition. It plagued him until his dying day. It might have been possible to bring back a man from the dead, if the hangman (hanging was the penalty imposed by the state for murder in Illinois) had merely suffocated his victim instead of snapping his neck, too.

Medics like Dr. Ben Casey and Dr. Kildare might try to resuscitate a suffocated victim but take a "hands-off" attitude if the neck had been broken. Unfortunately for Howey, the hangmen in Illinois did a thorough job in their specialties. All of their victims ended up in the morgue.

When William Randolph Hearst, Howey's boss, sent him to Boston in 1923 to infuse some much-needed blood into the veins of the slowly ebbing Hearst properties, (the *Boston Record-American-Sunday Advertiser*) Charles MacArthur, Howey's erstwhile employee, was already gainfully employed elsewhere. Although Howey wanted MacArthur to work for his newspaper, he couldn't afford the huge salary he commanded. It was then that Charley thought of a plan they had both hoped to enact back in the Windy City.

Boston was ideal for the "resuscitation" story according to Charley. "The Hub of the Universe," as the Chamber of Commerce terms Boston, didn't go in for hanging, but electrocution instead. As a trained reporter, MacArthur learned that the body could be claimed by the next of kin whenever the warden deemed it permissible.

A young Greek named Paul Pappas, accused of stuffing his sweetheart's body into a furnace, was then awaiting the electric chair. This was MacArthur's intended resuscitation victim. He would not let Howey know this directly because Walter would make him leave the employ of his newspaper to go to work for him. His own newspaper would not go along with the weird idea, so MacArthur worked on a scheme of his own.

Charley worked out a deal with Jo Swerling, then a special writer for Howey and later a famous writer of screen stories and plays. Swerling approached Walter and told him that he would get all of the Boston rights to the story and that his "mysterious" friend (actually MacArthur; but he didn't tell this to Howey), was to retain all other rights.

"The Swerling-MacArthur team lined up a young doctor who had presumably revived a baby, born dead," reminisces ex-reporter Dorfman, who worked for Howey. "An under-

78

taker, whose establishment was next to the jail, was also contacted. The mortician lined up with the nefarious duo. Pappas' only relative, a brother, was contacted and told that one of his relatives from Greece was anxious to obtain the body after the electrocution. The proper documents were signed by the brother. All was in readiness. On the eve of the electrocution, both went to the apartment of the physician."

The rest of the story is such a series of seemingly incredible events that one can believe that "truth is stranger than fiction."

Expecting to meet a young nervous medic, MacArthur later said it was here that they met with their first unexpected rebuff. They encountered what seemed to be the whole roster of the Massachusetts Medical Society. Their young medical cohort had confided his exoteric experiment-to-be to several doctor friends, who, in turn, spread the word among fellow members. He had not only violated his pledge to Swerling-MacArthur, but the Hippocratic Oath, as well!

"It took literally truck loads to haul all of the doctors to jail," added Cappy. "Two rode with MacArthur and Swerling in the undertaker's hearse, each holding huge hypodermic syringes full of adrenalin and saline solutions. While MacArthur waited outside in the reception room, Swerling went inside to witness the execution."

Suddenly, Swerling ran out, frantically shouting, "We're cooked!" and explained what had happened. The Chief Medical Examiner learned of their plan and had left a dinner party, still wearing his dinner coat and all to come to the execution. He brought with him a doctor-friend. He had asked his friend, a Doctor Smith, to examine Pappas' brain immediately after the electrocution!

The next day, according to Dorfman and the "Howey legend," MacArthur ran into Howey on Arch Street, outside of the *Boston American* offices. Walter asked him to dinner, hopeful he could persuade him to go to work for him.

"Look at all of the fun you'll have working for me. Only yesterday I had a terrific story you would have given your right arm to be working on," confided Howey. And he told him about the Pappas incident.

"MacArthur broke out in uncontrollable laughter," mused Dorfman. 'I know all about it. I was working the whole thing right under your nose,' he laughed."

Howey picked up a bottle of ketchup and broke it over MacArthur's head!

MOGER vs. HOWEY

"THE HOWEY LEGEND" is exceeded only by "The Moger Legend," which becomes increasingly distorted, especially at bars and taverns where newspapermen gather to recant fables about "the good ole days."

Luckily, my encounter with Howey was at a period when the one-eyed, inventor-newspaper editor was not in the prime of his life. Had it been, a bop on the head with a ketchup bottle, as he had once done to Charles MacArthur, would have been child's play. Not only did I almost cause him to lose his job as editor of the *American Weekly*, but I made him lose "face" with William Randolph Hearst, who never forgave him.

I served as Contest-Puzzle Editor for the Hearst newspapers in New England. After about a year on the payroll, the contests ceased and so did my job. Of course, in most newspapers the circulation department doesn't talk to the editorial department and vice versa. I still retained my office, working without pay, but using all of the facilities supplied by Hearst—gratis.

My father moved into the office, too. He had "retired" at an early age. The office at the *Boston American* proved to be his haven. He telephoned all his cronies and invited them up to *his* office. He greeted the elevator operators, daily; introduced himself as my father and arrived at the office at regular intervals every day. A busy man doing nothing.

The bulk of my business was as a free lance cartoonist. Many shows came to Boston prior to Broadway for tryouts. I was called upon, frequently, by the shows' press agents to plant stories in newspapers, draw caricatures of the players and get a column mention here and there. Being located inside a newspaper building had many advantages. I made the best of them.

Tom Weatherly, a well known New York press agent (he produced *The First Little Show* starring Fred and Adele Astaire, Clifton Webb, Libby Holman and Fred Allen), asked me to help exploit his latest assignment, a play called, *Higher and Higher.* He offered me fifteen dollars apiece for every cartoon that I placed in the newspaper, during its short run in Boston.

I prepared six drawings, each two inches wide by three inches deep. Each was titled: "Higher and Higher." Sample gags were: "The smallest room in the world is a mushroom." Or, "Did you hear the story about the three eggs?" ANSWER: "Two bad!"

Now you'll have to admit that this type of humor is not the best in the world. (Neither was the show, which featured a seal and Jack Haley.) But, ninety dollars was ninety dollars. Rent free, remember.

The drawings were refused by Jim Murphy, managing editor of the *Boston Record* and Win Brooks of the *Boston American.* My only hope was *The Boston Sunday Advertiser,* of which Walter Howey was managing editor.

I had my cartoons made into plates with no trouble. (Even

81

the engraving superintendent thought I was still in the employ of the newspaper.) I brought the plates into Howey and asked him:

"Do you mind if I show these drawings to Red Bowman? Maybe he could use them as fillers in one edition—the bulldog edition or the Canadian edition?"

These latter editions were a limited number of copies which were sent to the outskirts and out of state.

I am sure that he did not hear what I had asked, since he was hammering away like mad on one of the gadgets he was always inventing. Howey invented many gadgets for photography. His Howey Enlarger is used by photographers everywhere. He was also the first to transmit photographs electronically.

"Sure, laddie," he mumbled. (To this day I don't think he knew who was in the room, let alone what I had asked him.)

I went into the next room and told Bowman, one of the editors, that "the boss" had asked me to show him the cartoons and that I had the plates all made and ready to use for *one* edition of the Sunday paper.

I also promised Red a couple of free seats for the opening of *Higher and Higher*. This made more of an impression on him than the cartoons, I am sure.

Early Sunday morning, I scanned the pages of *The Boston Sunday Advertiser*. It was Easter Sunday. All of the Hearst editors vied for prizes offered by "The Chief," personally, for the best Easter Sunday magazine supplements. I beheld a beautiful section of the newspaper, replete with messages from His Eminence, Archbishop Richard J. Cushing and other spiritual leaders. Reproductions in full color of rare paintings from the Vatican were handsomely printed. Right smack in the middle of a message from a noted religious leader, I spotted a cartoon. It began . . . "The smallest room in the world is a mushroom. . . ."

The room began to spin around me! I felt sick! Probably not half as sick as Walter Howey. He got a long distance call directly from Hearst's San Simeon ranch. What Mr. Hearst told Mr. Howey has never been revealed. But, shortly afterwards, Howey was relegated to just a plain editor.

When I arrived at my "office" early on the following Monday morning, my father greeted me. He said I had just received a call from Mr. Jim Murphy, editor of the *Daily Record*.

What Mr. Murphy told me cannot be repeated!

I never spoke to Howey again. The next day, I was physically removed from the fifth floor of the Hearst building. Everything in my "office" was thrown out. This included three filing cabinets, two desks, three chairs (my father was asleep on one of them and they removed it so deftly that he didn't know he was in front of the building until he was awakened by a passer-by), an artist's drawing board and two typewriters. The funny thing about the whole episode was that *everything* they threw out, with the exception of us Mogers, belonged to them!

I HATE LAWYERS

WITH THE EXCEPTION of my brother, Nate (a true Perry Mason, who has never lost a law case except when defending me), I hate lawyers. Why?

Not too long ago I took a plane from Buffalo to Boston. Coming into Logan airport, I was the only passenger left on the trip. The stewardess brought me my coat. In the dim light I noticed a rough spot on the back of the jacket. I held it up to the light. There was a rip about a quarter of an inch in length. I showed this to the stewardess, who was in a hurry to get back to the pilot, and she said: "Oh . . . I must have caught it on a hanger."

"What do I do about it?" I asked.

"Take it to the Lost and Found Department at the American Airlines counter and they'll take care of it."

I went to Lost and Found and had one helluva time trying to find the attendant, who must have been lost, himself. He explained that it was late at night and he was only "filling in." However, he asked me to call a Mr. Ringer in the morning. I did. I explained my problem and asked him what was the next step. He told me to write a letter to the "home office," and to send a carbon copy to him. Also, at my convenience, to bring in the jacket.

A few days later I brought in my jacket. He looked at it and asked me if I had any objection if it were woven back to its original condition. Being a nice fellow, and having liked the suit, I agreed.

A few days later I received a call from Mr. Ringer. He told me, rather in a belligerent voice, that the jacket was a synthetic material and could not be woven. He was returning it to me with the rip.

I wrote to the airline's home office Claims Department. They answered. A nasty reply that in essence asked what assurance did they have that I didn't rip the coat myself and look to them for repair!

This got me to the boiling point. I called my learned Harvard '35, Harvard Law '38 brother (blood brother he calls me to differentiate me from just a plain shmuck "brother," as one lawyer calls another lawyer).

"Take the case, yourself, to the small claims court," was his sage advice.

I did so. I waited for the case to be called. Then brother Nate phoned me: "Guess what? The airlines wants a jury trial!"

"A jury trial?" I yelled. "Why those bastards can settle the whole case for twenty-five dollars if they want to."

Arthur Fiedler

Leonard Bernstein
Mitch Miller
Liberace

Julia Meade, Ed Sullivan

Danny Thomas

Top: Frau Moger, Danny Kaye, Ed Dukoff
Center: John F. Kennedy, Tab Hunter
Bottom: Bob Hope

So we waited until finally the case was heard before a Superior Court judge. As I entered the courtroom, a lawyer and a stenotypist appeared. I was cross examined, examined and further cross examined.

"What time was it when you arrived in Boston?" I was asked by the prosecuting attorney.

"About eleven-thirty P.M.," I answered.

"Was it dark or light when you arrived?"

Now if that wasn't the craziest question I had ever heard!

"It was light."

"Do you mean to tell me and the court that at eleven-thirty P.M.—almost midnight—it was light outside?" mocked the opposing attorney.

"Yes," I replied. "You don't think for a moment that American Airlines would allow its passengers to leave the plane in total darkness, do you? I say it was light *in* the plane and dark outside."

Turning to the judge the infuriated lawyer pleaded: "This witness is hostile. I ask the court to hold him in contempt. . . ."

So, I lost my head. The airline's lawyer refused to have the court present a copy of the letter I had written to Mr. Ringer, the day after I noticed the hole in my coat. The judge asked to read it. He meditated for a moment and said:

"I see nothing wrong with this. I'll admit it as Exhibit A."

He took the case under advisement. My brother was convinced I had "blown" it because of my temper. "Next time, don't waste my time and yours," was his warning.

A few weeks later Nate called me: "Guess what? You were awarded seventy-five dollars damages against the airline."

"When do I get it?" I asked.

"They have ten days in which to appeal the decision. They still have a right to take it before a jury. We asked for the trial not they. If we had lost then it would have been the end.

85

Since they lost they can still try again before a higher court."

Ten days later my brother Nate met in the chambers of Judge Edward A. Voke of the Superior Court. The airline wasn't giving up! Afterwards Nate told me what transpired there.

"How much does your brother want for the coat?" asked the judge.

"The lower court's Judge Canavan awarded him seventy-five dollars, Your Honor," said Nate.

"Well, tell your brother I'll give him seventy-five dollars to forget about this whole incident," said Judge Voke. Turning to the elderly lawyer, who was representing the airlines, a man who looked like Scrooge and acted like him, he said: "Henry, do you realize how much it costs to impanel a jury in this State? Why it's almost nine hundred and seventy-five dollars and for what? For a lousy rip in a coat? What's gotten into you?"

"I don't care how much it cost," said the airline's lawyer. "I think we can upset the verdict before a jury."

"You must be out of your cotton-picking mind, Henry. What do you really want?"

"Well," he drawled, "I want it to show that neither side won and I won't give him more than . . ."

"Do you want to give my brother fifty dollars and call the whole thing off?" Nate interjected. "We'll show that neither side won." (They used some karkemamia Latin phrase.)

"All right," said the airline lawyer, and both came out of the Judge's chambers.

The Judge shook his head. My brother walked out, carrying my coat with him. The original airline tag, which the stewardess had affixed to the coat when she hung it up, was fluttering in the breeze he made as he strode angrily toward me.

"Fer Chris' sakes, keep outta my hair and here's the god-

86

dam coat. You just got fifty dollars. I was afraid if he got you on the stand you'd say something and you'd wind up in jail for contempt. After all, you've wasted a whole day for me. Luckily, you can come and go as you please. Can you imagine a workingman taking all of this time off. For what? No honest citizen could afford to hire a lawyer and give up his time to fight such a silly case."

I took my jacket. I was going to give it to my janitor. After all, who would notice the tiny rip on the back. Maybe his wife could sew it for him. I would give him the pants, too. It was a beautiful black, lightweight, nylon suit.

Celebrating my victory, I bought a good cigar. I lighted it up and walked back to my office. I flicked the ashes. I smelled something burning. You're right! A big hole was smoldering in the pocket of the jacket, the airline tag still flying on the breeze.

Walking by a receptable which bore the legend: "Don't be a litterbug," I gently deposited the jacket with its quarter-inch rip on the back and its four-inch hole in the pocket.

I hate lawyers!

FREE LOADERS, U.S.A.

IT IS HARD to believe but there is a breed of citizens who eat well at night and sleep better during the day.

I call them "Free Loaders of America." I ran into one not too long ago at a meeting of motion picture distributors and exhibitors on behalf of an Israel bond rally. The principal speaker was a little fellow just returned from the State of Israel. His name was Herman Gilman. The affair was held at the Hotel Bradford, Boston. Tickets were priced at ten dollars each and every major film company was assessed for a table of ten tickets.

At my table was an ill-kempt, sweat-laden, dirty old man.

One of my neighbors turned to me and asked, "Who's your friend?"

"My friend?" I asked. "Why I don't know the sonovabitch and what's more I wish he'd change his seat. I'm going to move if he doesn't."

Turning to the unidentified guest I asked, "What theaters do you represent?" Now, you can't tell one stinking movie exhibitor from another. The fact that he was unkempt and badly dressed didn't mean that he wasn't a big theater owner. I've seen such characters in film row. They come in late model Cadillacs, park them a few blocks from the office of the film distributor, and come in crying while looking for an "adjustment" on a recently played film at their theater. The old adage of "crying all the way to the bank" originated here.

"Theaters, shmeaters?" he belched. "I came here because they are serving steak tonight." He pulled out a stained envelope and began reading: "At the Statler they got a big affair, but who wants chicken à la king again tonight? I had that yesterday. At the Sheraton Plaza they have two affairs. At one they are serving roast chicken and at the other roast beef! I feel like eating a good steak tonight."

"Howinhell are you going to get away without paying?" I asked. "Everyone has to turn in a ticket and since you don't have one, I assume, you'll get thrown out on your ass."

"What in hell do you care," he snarled. "Am I asking you to pay? Just mind your own goddam business, please."

I was curious to see how he was going to "beat the house" on this one.

When the waiters gathered around the tables, going from guest to guest, they tore off the lower half of the ticket that each guest had pinned on his suit. This was the ticket in payment for the dinner. When they came to my "friend," he said to the waiter: "I was asked here by the speaker. Get the ticket from him." With that he stood up and waved to Mr. Gilman. Gilman waved back. (What would you do if you were the head speaker and someone waved at you?) That's exactly what Mr. Gilman did. He waved back. We found out later he didn't know this character at all.

Food was served. The waiter went to the head table. A discussion ensued, but it didn't last too long. My "friend" was served, too. Obviously, the "house" picked up his check, because someone thought he was a friend of the principal speaker.

The man ate as if there was no tomorrow. It was obvious he enjoyed his steak. This is what he came for. When Mr. Gilman began to speak, my "friend" fell asleep. When Gilman was discussing the plight of the Jews in Israel he banged the desk with the gavel. The noise scared the fellow awake and he began to hiccough.

"Goddam lousiest food I ever ate. I'll never come here again." Hiccoughing, he made a hurried exit.

A few days later I attended a tribute to Richard Archbishop Cushing, now a Cardinal. It was at the Statler-Hilton Hotel. I was to meet Willard Matthews and some of the "boys" from Providence. The Variety Club was naming his Eminence "Prince of Peace" and presenting him with "The Great Heart Award."

Arriving a little early, I waited in the lobby for Willard and the others, including Al Clarke and Ed Fay, dean of exhibitors. Walter Brown, Chief Barker of Variety Club, walked over to me. "Why don't you go get a drink and some hors d'oeuvres while you are waiting?" I walked upstairs to the Parlor Room. There was no one there. "It is early," I thought.

I ordered a drink. I nibbled on some peanuts. I ordered another drink. Soon people arrived wearing formal attire, black ties and tuxedoes, with their women dressed in the highest evening fashion. "These must be invited guests," I thought to myself. "Friends of the Archbishop's, no doubt." I didn't recognize a soul. From the corner of my eye I saw Otto, the maitre d'. Here was the only familiar face.

"Hello, Mr. Moger," said Otto. "I didn't know you were a member of the 'Oogaloob Society'!"

Then Dr. Danny Miller and his wife, Rosa, came up to the bar. "What are you doing here?" I asked. Danny is an ear-eye-nose and throat specialist. "Possibly Danny knows people in show biz," I muttered to myself.

"I could ask you the same question," Danny grinned and left me to chat with his friends.

I walked outside to see if Matthews and the gang had arrived yet. I then saw that the card outside of the Parlor Room read:

Annual Meeting of Otolaryngologists (Eye, Ear, Nose and Throat Specialists).

I had walked into the wrong room.

I don't qualify as a "Free Loader of America." You have to get a free meal with malice aforethought. Accidents don't count!

PART THREE

laugh along with moger

> *"Laughter is anything which seems funny to me"*
> —Steve Allen

MOVIE PUBLICISTS GET TO SEE LIFE IN THE RAW, OR WHAT GOES ON BEHIND THE SILVER SCREEN

ONLY A FEW YEARS ago when I was in Hollywood, I was invited to a surprise birthday party for a beautiful unmarried movie actress . . . whose name I'll have to drop. Everyone of note from famous directors to prominent producers had been smuggled into her home by her boy friend, an equally famous and handsome leading man. The movie capital's upmost crust, top actors, writers and executives were there. A circular staircase was in the center of the downstairs living room. Our hero went to the foot of the stairs and called:

"Darling, come down, I have a surprise for you!"

Everyone held his breath. Diamonds glistened, minks bristled.

"Oh, it's you, dear," the actress called from her bedroom upstairs. "Hurry! I've been waiting for you, too, darling."

"Please come down."

"No, dearest. YOU come up! Wait until you see what *I have for you!*"

"No," cautioned the actor. "YOU come down, this very instant. Do you hear me, dearest?"

There was a silly giggle from upstairs.

"You *know* I have something that you want!" she sang.

A ghastly smile fell over the face of our hero as he tried to make light of the conversation to the vast gathering of guests.

"If you come down," he chanted back, "maybe I have an even greater surprise for YOU!"

This released the suspense. For a brief moment there was a hush and a foreboding silence. Then . .

"Here I come!"

And she did. She flew down the bannister of the staircase. She aimed directly at her anguished boy friend. Her arms landed around his neck.

Stillness marked the occasion.

"Happy birthday!" one of the crowd meekly said.

The rest just stared.

She was stark naked!

Then there is my favorite yarn about an actress who came home early one afternoon. Her hubby had been playing tennis in back of their home. The husband and his friend (not Moger, alas) had finished a few strenuous sets and then went back into the house to take showers. When the actress unlocked the front door and got no answer to her "Hello, is there anyone home?" she dashed upstairs. She heard the shower running and shook her head knowingly. Running into the bathroom, she put her hand through the shower curtain and grabbed.

"Ding dong, daddy!" she chirped. "Supper's ready!"

There was a gasp of not complete dismay. Giggling happily she started downstairs and met her husband coming up!

Jack Sharkey, Jack Dempsey

John Wayne, Ward Bond

Abbott and Costello

Rocky Marciano

Phyllis Kirk

Jack Webb, Dorothy Towne (Mrs. Webb No. II),
and Police Commissioner Thomas F. Sullivan

Jerry Colonna, Cary Grant

Fred Allen

COME UP AND SEE MY HOROSCOPE

"COME UP AND SEE MY ETCHINGS," has given away to the more trite term of "Let's compare horoscopes," says *Variety* editor, Abel Green.

Jupiter, Uranus, Virgo and Libra, with plenty of Taurus (the bull) seems to have taken over Hollywood. Many believe that Hollywood's self-styled No. 1 Astrologian is Carroll Righter, who relieves most of the movie stars from their anxieties.

He once predicted that Marlene Dietrich would break her leg in a studio accident. Dietrich swears by him ever since his prediction came true. She will not use an airplane unless Righter says it's "Okay to fly."

Among those who would rather be "Righter" than "wronger" are: Arlene Dahl, Robert Cummings, Rhonda Fleming, the Gabors, Adolph Menjou, Red Skelton, Susan Hayward, Hildegarde Neff and others.

Some Righter devotees call him "when they should go to the bathroom" according to one Hollywood star.

He has no monopoly on the Zodiac votaries, since some go elsewhere for their astrological advice.

Occasionally, Righter will meet his match with someone who is well versed in the signs of the stars. To Marilyn Monroe, he said: "I know . . . you're a Gemini. Did you know you were born under the same sign as Rosalind Russell, Judy Garland and Rosemary Clooney?" Marilyn is purported to have looked him straight in the eye and answered, "I know nothing about those people. I was born under the same sign as Ralph Waldo Emerson, Queen Victoria and Walt Whitman."

Carroll Righter drifts among his guests recalling their "signs" rather than their names. "Hello, Taurus," he says. "Hi there, Sagittarius." To his intimate friends he greets them with, "Hello, March 19 or July 1 or May 10." Once he met a woman and said, "Hello, March 27," then he turned to his companion and whispered in her ear, "What's her name?" He had forgotten an indomitable Aries: Gloria Swanson.

Most Hollywood stars prefer to be under the most famous sign of them all — NEON!

SPEAK FOR YOURSELF, JOHN!

IN ALL of my many years as a movie-goer, I have sat through thousands of motion pictures. Some have lasted for hours on end without interruption. One film made by Alfred Hitchcock, *The Rope*, was unusual in that it took in the entire action during the running time of the film. Yet, in all of these hours spent in the dark, I have never seen a movie star go to the john . . . on the screen, that is. True, they are a strange breed, but do they have cast iron bladders and delayed peristalsis?

Maybe we mentally endow these actors and actresses with God-like qualities which makes them unlike ourselves. Men like Hugh Troy campaign relentlessly against sham and smugness. Why? Hugh isn't sure, but he recalls that when he was a small boy he received a terrible shock when he discovered that people are often not what they seem. Pearl White, the famous serial queen of the silents was in Ithaca filming an episode of *The Perils Of Pauline*. The Troy lad worshipped her and did his best to get near Cascadilla Gorge where the scenes were being shot. He was constantly being chased away, however, and then one afternoon he was playing in the front yard of the Troy home on Oak Street. Up the street came the famous red Stutz roadster driven by the great heroine, herself. She stopped the car directly in front of the Troy house. The boy stared at her in disbelief . . . she was

94

smoking a cigar! She hopped out of the roadster, swaggered up the lawn and said:

"Hey, kid, kin I use yer terlet?"

It was too much. He ran weeping into the house, completely disillusioned by the knowledge that Pearl White had to go just like other people.

SOME OF MY BEST FRIENDS ARE ART LOVERS

MY GOOD FRIEND, Ben Schwalb of Sid Curtis' *Revere Journal,* wants me to know that the title of my book was *almost* the title of a columun by Bill Slocum, fellow fourth estater, in the *New York Mirror.* Bill's story was about someone else's experience.

I tell another man's story here. I tell it without comment. I doubt that any comment is possible.

"This man returned from Austria told me he had come across an old friend. He asked the friend how he had fared during the war and the friend replied, 'They put me in a concentration camp in nineteen hundred and forty-three. But it could have been worse. The German guards treated me well. Or better than they treated the others.'

"The man asked his friend how he had accomplished this miracle of decency on the part of the concentration camp guards. The answer was, 'I carved statues for them. Dozens of statues. All of them wanted the same thing.'

"And what was it that all the German concentration guards wanted?

"The fantastic answer was, 'Statues of Jesus Christ.'"

THERE, BUT FOR THE GRACE OF . . .

BENNINGTON COLLEGE is noted for many things. It is one of eleven U.S. campuses that have an ideal "intellectual climate" in the opinion of Syracuse University Psychologist George G. Stern. The other ten campuses include: (alphabetically, of course) Antioch; Bryn Mawr; Goddard; Oberlin; Reed; Sarah Lawrence; Shimer; Swarthmore; Vassar and Wesleyan University.

Located in Bennington, Vermont, where the sap comes from, it also is famous for:

(1) Two illustrious alumnae—or students who wished they were alumnae—comedienne Carol Channing (*Diamonds Are a Girl's Best Friend* and *Hello Dolly*) and Joanne Woodward (Mrs. Paul Newman), an Academy Award winner for *Three Faces Of Eve.*

(2) Diane Varsi, who ran here from Hollywood when she started to feud with 20th Century-Fox studios.

(3) My daughter, Roz, a graduate. (It is among the most expensive womens' colleges in the world; annual room and board plus tuition is more than $3,000 per annum.)

(4) It is near Williams, the Ivy league school.

(5) It overlooks a toilet-paper factory.

(6) It will never forgive itself for making the all-time "booboo" of its thirty-year existence when it refused admission to a bricklayer's daughter from Philly because they couldn't see "eye-to-eye" when she presented her credits and qualifications in high school mathematics.

Anyone knows that "One Princess equals one sizable endowment."

But someone goofed when Her Serene Highness Grace of Monaco applied for admittance to the college in Bennington, Vermont.

Alas, poor school! No rich Princess to look for at the annual reunion.

LETTERS . . . LETTERS . . .

HAVE YOU NEVER met a fellow who says: "I just wrote a letter to the editor . . ."? You don't have to be a college graduate to be a "Man Of Letters."

One of the more popular segments on the Perry Como Show was a feature called: "Letters . . . Letters," which dealt with "request numbers."

My cousin, Henry J. Stein, and his dad, Simon, like to write letters to the editors. As a matter of fact they both have voluminous files at their law offices captioned: "Letters of Little or No Importance." Editors will tell you that "Letters to the Editors" are as widely read as the obituary columns and want ads. In that order.

A funny letter came across my desk. It was sent to me by a friend who read about it somewhere. I can't vouch for its authenticity. It was written to Liggett & Myers in Richmond, Virginia.

"I've been smoking Chesterfield cigarettes for some seventeen years now, ever since I first tried the awful weed. As much as one can be satisfied through this narcotic habit, I must confess to my own satisfaction, in general, with the product you put out. I do, I must admit, change around from brand to brand for an occasional change of taste, but always come back.

"My gripe at the moment is that I have occasionally run across an individual pack (packed in a carton) which gives off a bit of a horse-shit aroma. Having spent some years of my youth on a farm, I must say that I am a bit partial to the odor of horses and even their evacuations (when a horse does pass, so infrequently these days, on the streets of New York, I will cross his path—behind him—to get a wholesome sniff) but I keep wondering if this is the kind of odor one should find in the blue smoke of a cigarette.

"Please check your hired hands. . . ."

Liggett & Myers presumably replied:

"We thank you for your letter of recent date regarding the taste of Chesterfield King Size cigarettes.

"While we appreciate your interest in writing us, we are at a loss to understand the condition and wish to assure you that there has been no change in the fine quality of the tobaccos used in our cigarettes. Every precaution is taken in the manufacture to make sure that the cigarettes leave the factory in good condition.

"We regret your experience and, under separate cover, we are mailing you a few packages. It is our hope that you will continue to enjoy smoking Chesterfield King Size cigarettes."

When *Playboy* magazine ran an advertisement for their "Femlins" (nude, white-bodied, and wearing long black stockings and gloves—with hair to match) *I* wrote to the Editors:

"I would appreciate three sets of your Femlins. Live please! One for myself, one for my son and one which I may be able to give away as a Christmas gift to a friend. How much are they?"

A few days later I received the following reply:

"The funniest thing happened on the way to the post office. We had your personal 40-25-38 Femlin Playmates all wrapped when we realized we forgot to enclose feeding and watering instructions. Next thing you know, they raised a fuss about being transported without proper directions for assembly and use in service. When we have straightened out this problem we will try to make shipment."

I still think they didn't try hard enough!

Anyone knows a live Femlin doesn't eat *that* much!

F.U.N. MEANS FUN!

NO LONGER does the English language mean what it says. The word SHAPE does not necessarily connote Brigitte Bardot or Gina Lollobrigida. It stands for: "Supreme Headquarters Allied Powers in Europe."

Songs with titles like: "Do you CARE for me?" could be a commercial tune for the "Cooperative for American Remittances to Europe."

Did you know the EPIC means "Emergency Public Integration Committee"? To hit "the SAC" doesn't mean to "go to sleep," for SAC designates the "Strategic Air Command."

I know of an organization which was formed to fight nuclear fallout. It was called "Save Humanity In Time." An alternate name was quickly discarded, too. It was tentatively known as: "Fallout Uncovers Considerable Knowledge."

Which brings us to the erudite observation of WHDH–TV's news editor, Joe Levine, who swears he knows of a government bureau, rightfully named "CAIC," which means, according to Joe, "Christ, am I confused!"

I'd like to start a fun club to include all of the movie people I know: "Names Under The Stars."

SAILING, SAILING, OVER THE BOUNDING MAIN

SHOW ME a true expense account and I'll show you a liar or a great fiction writer. The "swindle sheet" has been one of the most abused privileges attending big businesses. Many boys higher up condone malpractice in this medium and make certain "allowances" to which they close their eyes. Such is the case in the movie business.

One film company decided that its salesmen were not visiting towns on days when they were supposed to, according to their expense accounts. A "smart" efficiency expert came up with an original idea. He instructed every salesman to send a postcard from the town he visited. This postcard would attest to his being in the specific town (so he thought) by the postmark on the postcard.

One peripatetic salesman was sending in cards every day from different cities, with regularity. Finally, he left his job and relocated in another part of the country. For several weeks after his job had terminated, the home office received cards postmarked from sundry towns. Each bore the inscription: "Just visited this city. Moving on to the next. Postcard follows." It was signed by the former salesman.

If a law is made, there is always someone to break it. This salesman was smarter than the efficiency expert. He had given a batch of postcards, all properly inscribed and signed, to local theatre managers in different cities. He told each one of them to mail one on certain days. The managers hadn't been advised that the salesman had left his job and were merely carrying out instructions. The main office was knee-high in postcards until remaining salesmen were asked not to send in any more postcards.

A friend of mine, who is still a field-man for one of the major motion picture studios, tells me that he has been getting away with an expense account which shows: Stateroom and boat fare to Providence, R.I. from Boston, Mass.—$70.00."

Since the Boston-Providence steamship line has been abolished for more than twenty years, this is indeed a feat. However, more incredible is that his New York office has never caught up with him. He tells them it takes more than three days to get to his destination. Actually, one can make the run to Providence via railroad in less than fifty minutes if the New York and New Haven runs on schedule. The fare is only $2.21 round trip. This field man puts in an expense account for $70.00, which includes cab trips to and from the pier, a stateroom, and "seasick pills."

Once he was "all shook up," by a call from his New York superior.

"Phil," the voice stammered, "we have an early opening in Providence. Can you hop a plane and get there by Thursday? Don't take the boat; we don't have much time. Today is Monday. Can you do it?"

"You bet I can!" replied Phil. He wasn't kidding. He got there that afternoon. Not by boat and not by train. He bummed a ride on U.S. Highway 1 and got there in less than an hour. It cost the company the usual $70.00 plus "extras."

This same character always put in for cab fare from his hotel to the bank to cash a check. One day, a meeting was held by his superiors and he was asked if he could arrange to have a personal check from a company executive cashed at the bank.

"Sure I can," he volunteered. His boss gave him the check and Phil came back within five minutes with the money.

"How did you get back so fast?" asked his boss.

"The bank is in the hotel building," answered one of the boys at the meeting. This eliminated the cab fares to the bank from that day on for this field man.

However, he still travels to Providence by boat. With a good wind, he can make it in three days at the customary cost of $70.00 with the usual items of: "stateroom, cab fare to and from piers, seasick pills, etc.," all listed and accounted for.

CALL ME 'PISHER'

THERE ARE CONTESTS and contests. People like the lure of something for nothing, even if it's only eyestrain.

In a small town, not far from Albany, a local radio station

101

announced that "something of value" was buried in the vicinity of its minor league baseball diamond. The clue stated that it was "near home plate." The next morning the listeners, thousands of them, had dug up the entire baseball park. They had even removed the seats in the grandstand.

Then there is the favorite contest, "Walk up to the Mystery Man, tap him with a newspaper and say: 'You are the Mystery Man.'"

This is a perennial contest, but it can be dangerous. I know of a metropolitan newspaper which launched such a promotion and for a solid week people were being accosted by perfect strangers. They would walk up and say: "You are the Mystery Man." They would then take out a wad of paper, sometimes soaked in brine—which made it equivalent to a baseball bat—then proceed to beat the beejesus out of you.

One morning the contest editor woke up with a bigger swollen head than the customers who sued and complained that everywhere they went some crazy bastard would walk up and whack the living daylights out of them, then holler: "You are the Mystery Man."

As a matter of fact, they still have it going on. I just heard it on the radio.

IN A LIGHT VEIN

MANKIND NEVER REALIZED what was in store for it when Benjamin Franklin discovered electricity. The outdoor electric sign, which is used to announce "Spectaculars" and ushered in the "name-in-lights" era, can play havoc with fancy advertising displays . . . when some of their neon tubing and bulbs burn out.

To wit: When the faulty wiring proclaimed "HOT SEX" instead of the Hotel Essex, Manhattanites flocked for blocks to view this unheralded display of bright lettering. Recently, a sign announced a new location for a ghetto, when it read "BOY JEW" instead of "Boylston Jewelry Co." on the corner of Boylston and Washington Streets, Boston.

The funniest faulty-lighted sign I ever saw was that of an upright neon at the Hotel Touraine, which advertised: "HOT URINE." Honest. I have a picture to prove it.

Peggy Cass, the comedienne, reports that when she went out opening night to see her name in lights in James Thurber's *Carnival*, she was dumbfounded. The letter "C" was unlit.

Casual visitors to Clarkston, Washington, could pick up the wrong idea about the community if fast repairs were not made to a huge sign. Burned out wiring left only three letters in the word "Business" illuminated. The sign read "Clarkston SIN District, Tourist Information."

Legend has it that a man whose legal name was Michael Zass, a well-known Louisiana confectioner, changed it to the shorter version of "Mike." He didn't need faulty electricity to attract attention. It was a common sight to see trucks running up and down the streets of New Orleans, with colorful signs reading . . . "For the best candies when in New Orleans—look up Mike Zass!"

THE VERB—"TO GOOSE"

"GOOSING" is the all-American pastime.

I borrow from H. Allen Smith's *The Compleat Practical Joker* for a comprehensive treatise on "goosing." He maintains that the most elementary of all practical jokes is the goose. It requires no money, no equipment, and a minimum of preparation and planning for it is usually a spur-of-the-moment, or moment-of-the-spur operation.

"The only man, to my knowledge, who has made any sort of serious inquiry into goosing is H. L. Mencken. In connection with his study of the American language, Mr. Mencken once appealed to the scholars of the nation to help him find the derivation of the word. He set down his findings in Supplement One of his masterworks, *The American Language*. From it I quote:

"One of the most mysterious American verbs is 'to goose.' Its meaning is known to every schoolboy, but the dictionary does not list it, as far as I know no lexicographer has ever worked out its etymology. . . . The preponderance of medical opinion, I find, inclines to the theory that the verb was suggested by the fact that geese, which are pugnacious birds, sometimes attack human beings, and especially children, by biting their fundaments. There is also the possibility that the term may be derived from the old custom of examining a goose before turning out to feed in the fields by feeling of its rear parts: if an egg could be felt it was kept in its pen for the day. . . . The question remains why one person is "goosey" and another is not. Some resent "goosing" no more than they resent a touch on the arm, whereas others leap into the air, emit loud cries, and are thrown into panic. One of my medical informants suggests the susceptibility is mainly psychic, and may have its origin in an obscure fear (and perhaps an infantile memory) of a sexual attack, but other authorities believe it is caused by physical sensitiveness and is psychic only by association. Meanwhile, every American knows what "to goose" means, though the term appears to be unknown in England and there are no analogues in the other European languages. . . . There was a time when a craze for "goosing" arose on the Hollywood movie lots, to the consternation not only of its victims, but also of their directors, who saw many a scene spoiled. One of its most assiduous practitioners was the late Douglas Fairbanks, Sr. When the other performers in his company became so wary of him that he was constantly watched, he took to hiding behind scenery and properties and operating stealthily with a long fishing rod. He was finally put down by threats of heavy fines from the front office."

. . . So much for goosing!

CREPITATION

ON FEBRUARY 31, 1946, the World's Championship Crepitation Contest was aired at the Maple Leaf Auditorium in Thunderblow, Canada. This was the first such contest held since the outbreak of World War II, the competition having been dropped during hostilities because all contestants were engaged in producing hot air for the propaganda divisions of their respective countries.

The Oxford English Dictionary defines "crepitation" as "a crackling noise; crackling. The slight sound and accompanying sensation caused by pressure on cellular tissues containing air. . . . The breaking of wind."

Crepitating is one of the oldest sports known to man, possibly dating back to the days of Adam and Eve. Recent findings by excavators in the ancient Babylonian city of Skratchahynae prove beyond a doubt that crepitating was carried on as a fine art many centuries before the Christian era. Professional crepitators were held in highest esteem, and one cuneiform inscription, found in the Temple of Itchitochus, stated that according to law, even if a famine occurred, all crepitators were to receive their usual allotment of lentils and cabbage.

The Golden Age of crepitation occurred in England during the reign of Queen Elizabeth. Probably the greatest crepitation virtuoso was Sir Walter Raleigh, whose prowess in this sport was immortalized in Mark Twain's little book, *1601*. In English competitions of that period, it was customary for the crowd to shower the winner with small coins to demonstrate

105

its admiration. It was from this practice that the English coin, the "farthing," got its name. In its original form, the word was without an *h*.

Primitive man made his first musical sounds by crepitating. In order to imitate and elaborate on the vibrant tones created by crepitators, an oboe-like musical instrument was invented in Germany in the nineteenth century. It was appropriately called the "Heckelphone." Richard Wagner was one of the first to employ the instrument in his orchestra. Always seeking new effects, he found it ideal for the solo passages in "Siegfried's Reinfahrt" in his great music-drama, *Gotterdammerung.* How wonderfully it could have enriched the wind passage in Mendelssohn's *Meeresstille und gluckliche Fahrt,* had the composer only known of its existence!

Present-day crepitation contests are held under the rules laid down some two centuries ago by the Earl of Whiffingham, whose admirable book, *Crepitating Made Easy,* is so detailed and complete that it is more than eight inches thick, even though it is printed on the finest, thinnest tissue. In it are discussed all the fine points of the sport, and all the terms like "trill-blow," "threep," "flutterblast," "flooper," "plotcher" and "fundusbreak" are defined and described in the minutest detail, with many suggestions as to how to produce various effects. The addition of such fine points as directional crepitating, and the use by the judges of a stop watch and an audiometer to measure accurately the length and volume level of each contestant's effort, have not changed the sport very radically.

So great was the interest shown in the contest between England's Lord Windesmear and Australia's Paul Boomer that, immediately after the conclusion of the broadcast, the network offices were deluged with requests for a recording of this exciting match. Today, it is available at selected music stores which specialize in fine stereo and hi-fi recordings by such stellar artists as Belle Barth, B. S. Pully and Pearl Williams, to mention only a few.

It might be added here that the champion Lord Windesmear lost the match to challenger Paul Boomer when he accidentally crepitated too vociferously and "lost control" in full view of a packed auditorium. This was preceded by throwing away a "freep," worth only one point in competition, when he let one go right in the face of his challenger, as an act of defiance. Quelle d'hommage!

During the course of this match, records reveal a follow-up "flooper," the second time in the history of this sport that a follow-up "flooper" was achieved in open competition.

The only other time was during the World Series held in Europe in 1783. During the course of this series, Francois Phouphe (pronounced "Foof"), the famous French farter, after leaving a follow-up "flooper," defeated Sandy McWind, his Scottish opponent, by only one "bloop" and then dropped dead! In honor of Monsieur Phouphe the "bloop" has been dropped from open competition. A "flooper" counts ten points. However, a follow-up "flooper," a very difficult maneuver, counts forty points.

Memories may be stirred as one recounts the unusual talents of such stalwarts as Lord Windesmear, and Paul Boomer, who won the crepitation championship of the world one memorable night in February 31, 1946.

LADIES, BE SEATED!

DURING WORLD WAR II good Scotch and other office "luxuries" were hard to come by. However, there was no shortage of good liquor or Bourbon in the offices of Warner Bros. New York executives. Many concealed their bottles in locked cabinets. Keys to these cabinets were carried around on their person, and guarded zealously.

One morning an important sales executive, who needed a quick drink to shock him back to reality, reached for his precious liquid and discovered that the lock had been tampered with and that the bottle was half empty. He couldn't understand where the contents had gone since the bottle was almost untouched the night before.

Again, the next morning he noticed that the bottle was nearly empty.

Calling in one of the trusted WB employees, who had served as head of the Pinkertons early in his nefarious career, he was instructed to leave the cabinet door ajar, so that the liquor would be in full view of the mysterious culprits. Adding a colorless and tasteless liquid which had potent medicinal qualities to the contents of the amber fluid, they waited. Results came the next day when three painters who were decorating his offices failed to show up for work.

When they did arrive, they were wan and pale and couldn't understand why they had had diarrhea for three days running. The crime was solved and the "cathartic-containing" liquor was never touched by them again.

This brings to mind a story that John Huston swears is true. Louis "Satchmo" Armstrong had an interest in a weight-reducer called "Swiss Kriss." His slogan was: "The more you shit, the thinner you git. No shit!" John Huston told me that when Armstrong and his Jazz Band went to England that the Duke of Kent, an Armstrong devotee, became a "Swiss Kriss" user at Louis' insistence. According to Huston, the only time that the Duke missed attending important Parliament sessions was when "Satchmo" and his band came to play in England. The Duke, too, looked pale and dehydrated. Those in Buckingham Palace say that the royal "john" was in constant use by the Duke. Several empty cans of "Swiss Kriss" were in evidence in "Ye Royale Medicine Cabinet."

Along the same vein is the story about Harry Browning, the dean of Boston tub thumpers, who was prescribed a large dosage of prune juice and a laxative to relieve frequent headaches. He hired a cab to take him from his Scollay Square office to the Met Theatre for a meeting with leading movie magnates. Dressed in his best white suit and late for the meeting, he offered the cabbie an extra two dollars if he would get him to the theatre in time.

The cab driver spared no gas as he headed for the theatre. En route, he accidentally hit the curb and shook up Browning. Harry paid the extra two bucks to "clean up the cab" and those who saw him say he stealthily backed into the theatre and called for a new change of clothing.

A white horse "stole" the show from some big names, one afternoon. During a matinee performance of *At Home Abroad* at the Shubert Theatre, I attended the performance to draw some caricatures of the principals including Bea Lillie, Bert Lahr and Mitzi Mayfair, the dancer. Miss Lillie dressed as Kirsten Flagstad sat atop a white stallion. As she hit a shrill note the horse "ad libbed" all over the stage. It was minutes before the gin-playing stage hands backstage got their cue to ring down the curtain, amidst gales of laughter and much embarrassment.

The first act ended with the noise of brooms, shovels and mops being heard from behind the curtain.

This was one ad lib that was hard to follow, even for seasoned comedians like Lillie and Lahr.

W.W.B.

I WORKED for an incredible man at Warners. His name was W. W. Brumberg. Someone best described him as "looking like a head waiter and not a good one, at that!"

Bald, immaculately-tailored, he could get involved in more "situations" than a barrel of monkeys . . . all his own fault.

I once visited him in his New York office. His was the most frequented by the executives. He held the key to the executive washroom.

"Shut the door behind you," he whispered. I knew that something unusual was about to happen.

"I have just learned that Dumont Television has a gimmick which makes a black and white television into a color set. All you have to do is replace a two-dollar tube. Only the U.S. Army knows about this," he said.

He pressed the intercom button on his phone. He said to his secretary: "Marge, get me Dumont, right away."

The phone rang a few minutes later. He asked me to pick up the extension.

"My name is Bill Brumberg of Warner Brothers. I understand that you people have a new tube which can make a black and white TV set into a color one, for a few dollars. Don't ask me how I know but I know. Now, what I want to confirm is if you replace the RC 6-789-045-370 K tube with an AM 819-0620890 BK will that do the trick?"

"Howinhell would I know?" said the man on the other end of the phone.

"How dare you say that to me?" shouted W.W.B. "Warners pioneered sound and if it weren't for us, you wouldn't even be working today. We are the originators of what is now television. I'll have your job for this. My boss knows your boss and if he ever heard that you talked that way to me why you'd be fired on the spot. Who am I talking to?"

"The janitor of the Dumont Apartments," the voice answered, slamming the phone.

W.W.B. blanched. He had reached the Dumont Apartments instead of Dumont Television Studios.

After all, the secret was so great that he forgot to tell his secretary that there was more than one Dumont in the telephone book.

How was she to know?

COME CLEAN!

ANOTHER "BRUMBERG-ISM" deals with the time that his wife, Jeannee Golda, was visiting her sister in Cleveland. Bill had figured out a way to save on his telephone calls to her. It would also serve to tell her that he was feeling well, his high blood pressure and other ailments, real and imaginary, not withstanding.

Dave Garroway was doing his *Today* show from the NBC Studios at Rockefeller Center. The cameras would pick up his huge audience, mostly people en route to work. Many of these people would flash signs, wave and ham it up.

One day, a mysterious voice kept shouting: "Hygiene! Hygiene!"

Jack Lescoulie, the announcer, and other technicians affiliated with the popular morning program couldn't figure out this sudden acclaim for "cleanliness." Even associate producer, Les Colodny, was at a loss to explain the sudden mumbling of "Hygiene! Hygiene!"

Finally, the TV camera revealed our W.W.B. waving frantically and shouting: "Hi, Jean. Hi, Jean."

He saved on a long distance call to his wife, who had been foretold by letter to be watching *Today*. The program was also given a "clean" bill of health by W.W.B.

WATCH OUT BELOW!

THE PHOTO EDITOR of the *Boston American* was Jack Dixon. He's a hale and hearty fellow, coming from a long line of photographers. His dad was a well-known Boston newspaper photographer and he has two brothers serving on metropolitan newspapers.

Jack sailed to Tahiti with Sterling Hayden, and eventually ended up in Hollywood as a cowboy actor. Not unlike Hayden, he couldn't stand the insecurity of acting and returned to his newspaper career in Boston. His usual haunts were along T–Wharf, where he maintained an apartment.

At one of the local saloons, Jack made the acquaintance of a rich businessman who volunteered to drive Jack back to the T–Wharf apartment. It was hard for Jack to believe that a liveried chauffeur waited for them outside the tavern in a shiny black limousine. But it was true.

The chauffeur opened the door of the limousine and Jack stepped in, followed by his benefactor, and sat in the back of the luxurious car.

Jack gave directions to the driver who was unfamiliar with this quaint section of Boston. Arrived at their destination, Jack opened his door and stepped out onto the wharf. His rich friend opened up the other door and fell twenty feet into the icy waters of Boston Harbor!

PART FOUR

press agentry in twelve hard lessons!

"He who laughs last—didn't get the joke in the first place!"
—Walter Winchell

PRESS AGENTRY

DICK MANEY, the theater press agent-extraordinaire once said: "Press agentry is a heinous crime for which the Napoleonic Code hasn't meted out a just punishment. If you have a winner there is nothing you can do to hurt it. If you have a stinker you can hide diamonds under the seats in the theater and no one will come to look for them."

I don't agree with him. I have seen many a film destined for the junk heap suddenly become a blockbuster because it was "made" into a winner. So it is with talent. Who knows where another Elvis Presley may be lurking? (So, who cares?) Or a Perry Como or Bing Crosby or a Fabian or a Marilyn Monroe?

One day, years ago, Harold Krensky suggested to me:

"Art, I just heard a great singer at the Fox and Hounds Club. Her name is Marion Francis. She has a pair of pipes that you can hear clear across the country. She's beautiful and needs an agent. I told her that you have some contacts with George Abbott. He's casting for a new show, *Beat The Band*. She would be great in it. Let's bankroll her trip for an audition. It will cost us about fifteen dollars each. We can wind up with half of her earnings. She's already signed a contract with me designating both of us as her agent. How about it?"

I agreed with his proposal. We were on the threshold of fame and fortune.

Now fifteen dollars was fifteen dollars in those days of my youth. We pooled our monies and I accompanied Marion Francis to New York. I had arranged an audition for her. George Abbott and I sat in the darkened theater. For atmospheric aid there was a single giant light bulb, dangling nakedly overhead. The stage looked like a burnt-out fireplace.

By Abbott's rules, each girl vying for the starring role in *Beat The Band* was allowed eight bars of music of her own choice. At the call of her name, a girl had a split second to break from the backstage jam, shuck her bandanna or other raiments, deliver her music to the pianist, and warble or belt out her song.

Marion was called. Gazing back from the auditorium into the blinding wattage, the men sitting alongside George Abbott in judgment must have thought: "It's like looking into the eye of God." I'm sure Marion thought so, too. For out in the dark sat the people who could make her Broadway's biggest star. And, also lots of money for herself, Krensky and Moger.

She took her place on center stage. She opened her mouth to sing and she began to croon—soft, dulcet, inaudible notes wafted across the darkened footlights.

"Next!" shouted Mr. Abbott.

"Wait till you hear her give out. She has a pair of pipes

114

which will shatter the chandelier in this theater," I cautioned George.

"I've heard enough. She's strictly a microphone singer," he added.

We never did find out why with a voice like hers that Marion had selected a song which began very softly. Eight bars. All of the time allotted her and Marion struck out.

Over the years, many "talents" are offered me. I turn them down. I am not in the talent scouting business. It is too time consuming and is highly specialized.

One day, Marilyn Goffstein, a roommate of my daughter, Roz', in Bennington College, called me. She told me she had heard a trio of singers who wanted a "manager." I could hear them singing in an off-beat Boston night club, which catered to beatniks. I told her I wasn't interested and thanked her for her innate knowledge of "good talent."

I forgot about them until one day Marilyn told me the trio was known as "Peter, Paul and Mary."

A few years ago a fellow came to me and asked me to draw an insignia for a male singing group he was handling. "They'll be bigger than the Kingston Trio," he told me.

"Sure," I agreed with him.

"We can't afford to pay you for the art work you are doing for us," he said, "but when they make a record I'll send you one. If you want to, I think I can arrange so that you can have a 'piece' of them, if you want to handle their advertising publicity, etc."

"No, thank you," I said. "I'll take the money."

He should have insisted. The Limelighters became America's number one male trio!

Then there was the time that C. O. D. Gordon, a jeweler, pleaded with me to handle his grandson, Barry Gordon. How did I know that Barry would end up starring in *A Thousand Clowns.*

A press agent doesn't believe the press clippings. He might have written them, himself!

I am now trying to launch the career of a handsome, six-foot three giant of a man, named Chuck Connors. He's a fine singer and a good guitarist. He's in his early twenties. He is a former "Mr. New England" and a "Mr. Universe" contender. He also has muscles on his tonsils.

Ten to one you've seen him on TV!

THAT'S GRATITUDE

"ALL THE GRATITUDE you find in Hollywood can be put into a gnat's belly button with enough left over for an agent's heart and three caraway seeds," thus Fred Allen, cynically described the film capital to me.

I found out that he was right.

The name Eugene Carey may mean little or nothing to you. He was an ex-marine, living near New Bedford. He was a tall, pock-marked, confused fellow, who was writing a book. Married comfortably, he was re-living his experiences of the war. An uncle, an insurance broker, brought Gene to a local theater one evening. The owner-manager said to him: "Gee, you're a handsome guy. Why don't you get into the movies as an actor?"

"Fine. *You* get me into the movies."

I received a call from the manager-owners, Harry-Mort-Fisher Zeitz, three brother theater owners in New Bedford.

"We have a new star for Warner Bros.," they each screamed into their own telephone extension. "We're asking him to contact you."

I had nothing to do with talent scouting. I told them that if they were expecting a fire in their theaters to get a new insurance broker. Why bother me? They persisted and I told them to tell the fellow to send me a biography and a photograph of himself.

Two days later I received a biography of the "star" and a photograph taken at a five-and-dime store . . . yellowed and out of focus. It began:

"As a freshman in the University of Miami I played in *Sirranno de Bergerak*." This guy couldn't even spell.

Three days later the three mousketeers, Harry, Mort and Fisher came into my office. "What happened to *our* boy?" they asked in unison.

"Nothing!" I shouted back. "This guy's an idiot. Howinhell can I arrange for a 'screen test' for this guy?" and I shoved the tin-framed picture under their running noses.

"Oh, this guy is a handsome fellow," they chimed back. "This picture doesn't do him justice."

So, in a moment of weakness I called my New York office. I spoke to our talent man, one Arnold Hoskwith.

"If it means anything to you," said Arnold, "I'll send the guy a form letter and ask him to come to New York for a reading. We don't give any screen tests till we find out if the guy has a good voice."

I assumed this was a total loss.

Gene Carey called and asked me if I could handle him as an agent.

"Yes," I said, thinking all of the time what a waste of time it would be.

"Send down a sheet of paper, Mr. Moger," he said.

Carey went to New York. He read for the talent department. He gave them the best reading they heard in eight years. At that time John Wayne was making a film called *Operation Pacific,* with Patricia Neal. The second male lead was feuding with the studio over billing and salary. To put him in line they hired Carey. I didn't know about it until he was in Hollywood. The Zeitz brothers called me and told me that they asked Carey if he had an agent and he said: "I dunno. This guy Moger gave me a sheet of paper. I didn't sign it. What shall I do?"

They looked at the "contract" and told Carey, "Don't worry, we'll take care of Moger!" Moger is still waiting. . . .

Warners changed his name to Phil Carey. He went on to make many films.

I ran into him not too long ago, on the Warner lot.

He nearly dropped his tray when he saw me. The first thing he said was: "Hey, do you know of a *good* agent?"

Now, do you think he was kidding?

As Fred Allen said: "All the gratitude you find in Hollywood . . ."

NON ILLEGITIMI CARBORUNDUM

ABOVE MY CHAIR in my office hangs a printed card. It reads: "Non Illegitimi Carborundum." It is autographed by the late Bill Cunningham, noted writer-commentator, with the added note: "To Art Moger from one fellow member to another."

If you are an erudite scholar, this won't stump you. It is "pig-Latin" and means: "Don't let the bastards grind you down!"

I first saw it in the office of a down-Easterner lawyer. I think he lived up to this motto in every way. He put me to the test and luckily I survived.

It all happened back in the 1940's when I got a sudden call from my New York chief at Warner Bros. that a world premiere was in the offing.

"Go up to Skowhegan, Maine, wherever in hell that is. Case the joint and report back to me where we can have a world premiere of the new movie, *Life With Father*."

I wired the only three "hotels" in Skowhegan for a room

118

and a bath. Only the Oxford House management came back with a reply in the affirmative. I finally arrived in Skowhegan by train. I checked into the Oxford House, a hotel above the local five-and-dime store. It looked like a comical facade from a cheap western movie. The manager asked me if I recognized him. Now, whoinhell would I know in this God-forsaken two-bit hotel?

It was an old Boston buddy, Sid Stone, who had married the daughter of the head of the local Chamber of Commerce and was now a big shot, himself. He not only owned the Oxford House but had the only Western Union machine in the town. Every wire that ever came in or went out of the town had to come across his desk. He knew everyone's personal business—that is, if it was ever transmitted via wire. When I had sent my wire to the three hotels in the town, he knew I had asked all three. Since only two hotels had baths above the second floor, due to faulty water pressure in the town, and since the other hotel had refused me, he had me by the proverbial short hairs. Had it been someone else, he told me, he would have refused him. But knowing me to be a friend of long standing, he gave me a room in his hotel.

I told him what I was doing in the town. He looked at me as though I had three heads. "You're crazy," he began. "If you want to see the site where *Life With Father* first played as a summer stock company, you want Lakewood, Maine. It's only a few miles from here."

I hiked up to Lakewood, a summer resort replete with a lake, cottages, fishing, swimming, souvenirs, picnicking, and a theater where New York plays try out during the summer months. I went to the home of the Swetts. It seemed Mr. Swett was a street car conductor and his street car traveled the road to Lakewood. It stopped in this Garden of Eden to let off families out for a picnic. The woman who had owned this tract of land liked Mr. Swett. When she passed on, she

119

willed the land and its boats and concessions to him. He, in turn, had willed it to his daughter.

After many years, by ingenuity, luck and a turn in events, Lakewood became a mecca for tourists. It also became the haven for embryonic Broadway producers. One such team was Howard Lindsay and Russell Crouse. They wrote a play in 1939 called *Life With Father*. It became a smash Broadway hit. Warner Bros. paid a handsome, unheard-of sum for the picture rights. The stage play gave a little actor named Marlon Brando his first glimpse of the big time as one of the red-headed members of "Father's" family.

All went well. We paid thirty dollars per day for a cottage . . . per person. I had a motley crew of worthless workers from the WB stable, who spent most of their time swimming and trying to make out with the local girls. The Swetts had agreed to turn over their summer theater to us for one week in August for the world premiere of *Life With Father*. It was to take place at the same theater, exactly eight years to the date, from its original opening as a stage show.

Warners sent out invitations to critics and the press from coast to coast.

We had agreed to pay the Swetts for the use of the cottages, as well as to give them the world-wide publicity they were seeking. In addition, we would pay them a handsome sum for a clambake to be held on their premises; a flat fee for the use of their theater (for ONE night); allow them to use the equipment which we had transported from New York to make the summer theater a bonafide movie house. (We strung lights with special transformers, etc.) It was mutually accepted as a good deal.

I was visiting my son, Stan, in Potter's Place, New Hampshire where he was attending a summer camp. It cost me one thousand dollars for eight weeks to prove that my number one son could make a twenty-five-cent ash tray. Suddenly, I received a frantic telephone call from one Sid Cain, a fellow Warner-ite, whom I had left in charge of the preparations.

"Come back, Art," he fairly cried into the phone. "They are calling off the world premiere. The Swetts want a cool sixty thousand dollars to take care of their loss of business in the concessions, boat-leasing and summer theater receipts."

I hurried back to Lakewood where I was met by the Swetts' lawyer. Let's call him attorney Brown.

"You know," began attorney Brown, sucking on a broken-stemmed pipe, "we are only jes' plain folk heah and we know nuthin' about you city slickers. . . ."

"What do you mean?" I asked him.

"Well, you Hollywood folk seem to be the only ones that's gonna make any real money outta this picture-showin'. Now my clients, the Swetts heah, they don' realize that they stand to lose everythin'. Why don't you fellers take over the whole week's business at Lakewood Inn, what with the boats an' the postcard-sellin' an' Edward Everett Horton in his new play. You know this is the week of the Skowhegan Fair and this is our busiest season an' . . ."

I excused myself and called Messrs. Mort Blumenstock and Larry Golob, two of WB's directors of advertising and exploitation in New York. Blumenstock was a vice president whose salary was in the upper four figures per week. He was a red-faced, towering two-fisted fighter. Golob was a self-made publicist whose vocabulary consisted of four-letter words. He looked and acted like Humphrey Bogart.

The duo arrived in Lakewood, where I explained the sudden turn of events. We confronted slow-speaking, pipe-sucking attorney Brown. Brown had us over a barrel, since we had but a scant two weeks to put on the world premiere, as scheduled. Invitations had been sent out. Acceptances were being received daily from celebrities all across the country. Equipment was being rushed by every conceivable mode of transportation to this outpost of amusement.

"Well," drawled attorney Brown, "my client heah," pointing to the daughter of the late Mr. Swett, "wants the sixty thousand dollars before sundown or we call the whole thing off." He removed his eyeglasses and pretended to wipe them.

"Whatinhell are you standing here for?" bellowed Blumenstock at me. "You must be a chowderhead or something! Let's not put attorney Brown and his client to any more trouble than we have to. Go on down to the State Theater in Skowhegan. That's a regular movie house. We don't have to run any special wiring, bring in our screens, worry about all of the other problems of making over a summer theater into a movie theater. Maybe attorney Brown is right!" With that Messrs. Golob and Blumenstock started to leave. As a parting shot, Blumenstock said to attorney Brown:

"Thanks for doing us such a great favor. You have saved us untold time and expense. Go back to your boat business. Run your concessions. Sell your postcards and tell all of those people at the Skowhegan Fair that Edward Everett Horton is coming . . . in person, too. We'll pay you for the use of the cottages at thirty dollars per head and whatever food has been eaten will be paid for in full. Our boys have been here almost three months, during your off-season. However, we don't mind paying you the going season rates. That's how fair we want to be to you and your client."

"B-b-b-b-ut, g-g-gentlemen," gasped attorney Brown, turning beet red, "surely you are joking."

"Joking, my ass!" Golob snarled.

"Why, of course not," said Blumenstock. "You have gotten what you want. We have what we want. So, there can be no hard feelings. Right?"

122

"B-b-b-but all of the publicity you have had about the world premiere in Lakewood. How do you feel about that?" Brown asked nearly choking on his pipe.

"We made a mistake, that's all," Mort said coolly. "It's only a hop, skip and a jump. I'm sure we can arrange to pick up our guests at the railroad station in Skowhegan. It will work out better all around."

"Won't you let me discuss this with my client, gentlemen?" Brown pleaded.

Mort finally agreed.

A few minutes later the defeated attorney Brown and his client "gave in" to all of Blumenstock's demands. No boat-renting by Warner Bros. We would not undertake any of the liability or losses resulting from lack of postcard buying, summer rentals, Mr. Horton's new play, etc.

WB agreed to a bill for cleaning up the "grounds" after the premiere. We eventually got a bill for $3,000.00 . . . enough to clean up the whole State of Maine. Brown put everything down in writing, at our insistence, so that there would be no mistake made.

The premiere was a huge success.

A week later Mort called me into his office.

"You did a great job," he commented.

"So did you," I rejoindered.

"Take a look at the contract Warner signed with Lindsay and Crouse, before spending almost eight million dollars to make the picture." Mort handed it to me grinning.

I read it. My eyes widened.

One line stood out more than any other:

". . . and it is further agreed that the world premiere of *Life With Father* must be held on the same site where the stage play was first produced. If not, the play reverts back to the original authors and advance payments may be kept. . . ."

Had attorney Brown only known. He could have demanded and gotten a million dollars!

"Non Illegitimi Carborundum."

STOP THE PRESSES!

CAN YOU BELIEVE what you read in the papers?

A press release came across my desk about a beautiful playgirl bunny right out of Chicago's famous Playboy Club. She was Nancy Dusina, who had her fondest dream come true when she made her motion picture debut in American International Pictures' *Operation Bikini*. Nancy was spotted by James H. Nicholson, co-producer of the film and president of AIP, who happened to see her at the Playboy Club while visiting Chicago.

Now, you may wonder what brought Nancy to the Windy City? According to the press release, which must have been written by a witty press agent with tongue in cheek:

"Dark-haired Nancy is from Modesta, California, in the Golden State's famous San Joaquin Valley. She was raised and went through school in the valley and through one year in Cabrillo College of Watsonville. During her last year at school she worked one summer as a butcher and learned to do custom slaughtering and meat smoking. Since Chicago was the heart of the meat smoking industry she came to the city etc., etc."

Meat smoking?

A PRESS AGENT CAN DO ANYTHING!

STRANGE REQUESTS come across the desk of a press agent. One day, I received a call from Ben Kalmenson, then President of Warner Bros. Pictures. Mr. K. was in New York. Boston had won the American League pennant.

124

Left to Right: Dan O'Herlihy Jr., Mervyn LeRoy, Jean Simmons, Efrem Zimbalist Jr., and John Veitch

Burt Lancaster, Bill Hendricks, and Nick Cravat

Left to Right: John Huston, Patrolman Ray Berlo, Mr. and Mrs. Gregory Peck,
Bill Cunningham, Frederick Ledebur

Doris Day getting azaleas from Band Leader Les Brown as Irene Ryan
(Beverly Hillbillies), TV Producer Hy Averbach, Cartoonist Zack
(Smiling Jack) look on.

"Get me six tickets for every game in the World Series," shouted Mr. K. He usually shouted.

"Where am I going to get them?" I asked.

"That's your problem, not mine. Get 'em!"

Now when the President of the company that's paying you a handsome salary asks you to do something, you do it or else. . . .

I called in an assistant who knew every gambler and bookie in town.

"Phil, I want you to get me six tickets for all seven games from one of your bookie friends. Price is no object. Benny Kalmenson wants them."

With this order and command, Phil took off and soon returned with the toughest looking hombre this side of Pecos. He was pock-marked, bruised, cauliflower-eared and dressed like something out of a Damon Runyan tale.

"I want seventy-fi' dollars de pair o' tickets," he snarled. A little mathematics revealed this would be $225.00 for six tickets per game or a grand total of $1,575.00 for the seven games.

I called Mr. K. in New York. I told him the story. The bookie was waiting impatiently, tossing cigarette butts all over the floor in reckless abandon.

"What do yer guys say? Are yer buyin' or aincha?"

"Just wait," I said. "I have to find out where the money is coming from."

I asked Mr. K. where I would get the $1,575.00 to pay for the tickets. I don't usually carry more than two dollars with me.

"Ask Bill Horan to lend it to you!" shouted back Mr. K. Bill Horan was WB's branch manager. He was tighter than the skin on a Scotchman's bass drum!

"You must be outta your cotton pickin' mind," Bill said, when I told him what Mr. K. had suggested. "I don't care if

Kalmenson said so or not. Let *him* give it to you, if he's such a big sport!"

"Look, fellers," the bookie said irritably, "yer wastin' my time. If youse don' want the tickets say so and I'll blow I ain't got all day to hang aroun'."

I called Mr. K. back again and told him I couldn't get the necessary funds and that the bookie was impatient.

"Call Leo Forbstein, the musical director at Warners. Actually, they are for him. He called me and asked me to get him the tickets," said Mr. K.

I called Leo. The tickets were not for him but for his brother. I called his brother who lived in Texas. He didn't want the tickets but his son attended Harvard and would I be so kind as to call him. I called him. The tickets were not for himself. They were for his tailor. Would I mind calling his tailor? I did. The tailor wanted them at cost and for only one game.

I didn't have the nerve to tell the bookie. I left the office hurriedly. I called in from a pay station telephone and told Phil to tell the bookie the deal was off. I didn't go back to the office for the rest of the afternoon.

PECK'S BAD BOY

A PRESS AGENT's greatest asset is his lie-ability.

Occasionally, a press agent will fall into a situation which will catapult him and his client into national fame. Such was the case when Gregory Peck and John Huston came back to Boston from a weary but triumphant personal appearance in New Bedford's world premiere of *Moby Dick*. A short stop in Providence for the same film saw a weary troupe of an actor and a director with a press agent bringing up the rear.

"Make tomorrow's schedule in Boston an easy one, Art,"

pleaded the lanky Huston, as he adjusted his hound-tooth checkered cap on the side of his head.

"Okay, John. I'm tired, too. As it stands now we have a theater appearance for Greg and you and a tour of the Chelsea Naval Hospital."

I had arranged a tour of the hospital via Fred Cusick, a former radio announcer friend of mine and then a PR officer for the U.S. Navy. It was always good for morale building for those who were shut-ins and meant ample newspaper coverage. Fred, in his usual manner, had given the forthcoming p.a. by Gregory Peck and John Huston plenty of build-up in all the communications media.

When we finished the personal appearance on the stage of the Astor Theater, Boston, we sneaked Peck out of the back door into a waiting limousine. Huston was a little late. He was besieged by autograph hounds who were waiting for him.

"Call up the Naval Hospital and tell them we won't come," said Huston wearily. I went to a nearby phone to call off our pre-arranged visit.

A woman standing nearby heard Huston.

"You ought to be ashamed of yourself. You're nothing but a goddam 'Red.' You and all those Hollywood phonies try to get admiration by announcing you're going to visit the sick and wounded servicemen just to get some free publicity. My husband has been at that Naval Hospital for more than fourteen years. He called me last night and was all excited because Gregory Peck and you were visiting him and the boys. Just wait till I tell him and my friends what bastards you all are," she fumed.

Now you can call a Hollywood director a whore-monger, a pimp, wife-beater, homosexual, anything—but don't ever call him a "Red." To be classified as a communist is a fate worse than death.

Huston changed his mind. "You'd better tell the Naval officer friend of yours that we will visit the hospital. Who does she think she is calling me a 'Red'? Why I produced films for the army, without realizing a penny for my efforts. A 'Red,' am I? We'll see about that!"

I called the Naval Hospital but the Commander had already received my message about the cancellation. He had left the hospital in a rage. I was told he was infuriated at the change of plans.

As we returned to the hotel, I was called by a friend of mine at the Associated Press.

"You're making the headlines," he began. "I have a story filed by a Commander Smith (that's not his right name). He calls Gregory Peck and John Huston Hollywood-ites who use the servicemen to exploit their films, etc. It's a rough story. I won't use it but I'd suggest that you pacify the Commander because he can make plenty of trouble for you guys."

I thanked him and told Huston what had happened.

"We gotta go to the hospital, now," he moaned. "Get Peck and tell him I said so. Let's not waste any time!"

We all piled into our Cadillac, directed our motorcycle escort to rush us to the Naval Hospital. Sirens blasting we arrived in Chelsea in short order. We found that the gates at the Hospital were closed to us with orders not to admit us. I cajoled and pleaded with the guards to call the Commander and tell him that we had already arrived.

I called Fred Cusick. He had already heard what had happened from the Commander and told me to wait. Finally, the Commander and his staff arrived at the gates. He was cold to us. I explained to him that I had made a mistake on my schedule and thought our arrival was for the next day. He looked at me quizzically. Finally, he wavered and let us inside the gates.

Inside the hospital we were greeted by television cameras,

newspapermen and photographers. Bulbs popped as if a big story was in the making. It was, but I didn't know it!

Greg and Huston were ushered into a room. They came out looking as though they were ready to perform an operation, both wore the customary white masks and garb of Dr. Ben Casey.

The cameramen were all dressed in whites, too. They wore masks like Peck and Huston. They all went into a glass-enclosed room. This is the story of Judy White.

A little girl, fourteen years of age, she had gone downstairs from her bedroom to the kitchen of her home, in Ashland, Massachusetts, to heat some milk for her little puppy. A flame from the gas stove ignited her nightgown. Before she knew it, she was a veritable pyre. Now she was in the hospital with more than seventy per cent of her body seared with third degree burns. She was a beautiful girl. I could see her from the outside of the glass. Her face and jet-black hair luckily weren't even touched by the fire. Her dad was a Navy man and she had been admitted to this fine hospital because the doctors were experts in plastic surgery.

Peck looked at her. Tears welled up in his eyes. He was Judy's favorite actor. She smiled at him.

"Judy," said Greg, as he caressed her forehead and gave her a kiss on her cheek, "I want you to look in on me on Sunday on the Ed Sullivan Show. I'm going to talk to you and I want the whole nation to know who my real sweetheart is. Get well quickly and I'll be writing to you, often. When you get better, come to see me."

Huston also talked to Judy. "When you get better, darling, I want you for a part in my next picture, *Tahiti*. You are pretty enough to play in it. I'll wait until you get well enough to play the part. I promise."

We left the Chelsea Naval Hospital much happier than when we arrived.

Peck sent a television set to Judy's room. Huston sent her a gold charm bracelet replete with gold charms.

The following Sunday Gregory Peck addressed millions of Ed Sullivan devotees. He began, "Ladies and gentlemen, I don't have a prepared speech. A few days ago, I visited a little girl, who is my real sweetheart. Her name is Judy White. About a week ago she went to feed her little puppy some warm milk. Accidentally, her nightie caught fire and she was nearly burned to death. Today, she lies at the Chelsea Naval Hospital, Chelsea, Massachusetts, with more than seventy-two per cent of her body suffering from third degree burns, or worse. Won't you do me a favor? Please send a 'get-well card' to Judy? Her name is Judy White, Chelsea Naval Hospital. Good night, Judy, dear. Get better soon. I love you!" He blew her a television kiss.

In the next few weeks Judy received more than 160,000 cards and letters.

You know the rest. A press agent's "dream" story.

WHY A MOTORCYCLE POLICE ESCORT?

ONE OF THE BANES of world premiers is the motorcycle escort. Many cities now frown on the practice of police accompanying stars on these personal appearances.

In Buffalo, not too long ago, a pedestrian was run down by a motorcade which was transporting a teen-age screen idol from a broadcasting studio to his hotel. From then on, the Mayor made it known that police escorts for such events were taboo in Buffalo.

John Huston, Gregory Peck and I went to Providence to herald the opening of *Moby Dick*. Willard Matthews, then managing director of the Majestic Theatre, arranged to have four Providence motorcycle policemen meet my car at the boundary line of Pawtucket and Providence to insure us safe and speedy delivery to his theatre.

As we approached the demarcation line, sirens shrieked, motorcycles sputtered and what had been a serene ride turned into a chase reminiscent of a movie thriller. Pedestrians jumped out of the way of the speeding bikes, motorists pulled to a halt—some even jumped the curbs and landed on the sidewalk—wondering what in Hell was happening!

At the Majestic Theatre manager Matthews beamed in anticipation of our applause for this display of VIP treatment. Huston's remark deflated us all.

"Boy, I don't know how you knew it," said John, "but I have to take a leak badly."

SAM, YOU MADE THE PLANS TOO LONG

DR. FRANKENSTEIN created his monster, Louella her Parsons and Hedda had her Hopper. Me? I have my Sam Mitnik.

Sam Mitnik has been adopted by the motion picture industry as its greatest celebrity. He has been immortalized the world over, by H. Allen Smith in his bible for practical jokers, *The Compleat Practical Joker.* Columnists from far and wide call Sam "the man in the empty chair." He always sends his "regrets."

That's the way it's been all of his life. If you've never had the rare privilege of hearing about this fabulous little man, it's high time you did. This peripatetic big shot of the movie industry might happen to be the suave tycoon sitting in the empty chair next to you.

Sam is the Paul Bunyan of picture-land, the Baron Munchausen of filmdom. Where Kilroy has been, Mitnik never goes. In politics and world affairs he votes both sides of a two-party ticket and stands firmly in favor of the inevitable. He has been claimed as a native son by regions from Houston to Hartford. It's time now for somebody to get the authentic genealogy on the record.

Sam was born in Lakewood, Maine, on August 14, 1947, when the temperature was about 109 in the shade. On that day, critics and movie VIPs were gathering from all over the East for the premiere of *Life With Father*.

It had been a painful junket north, partly over a roadbed that hadn't been used in seventy years. The heat was stifling, the air-conditioning had broken down, the train had stalled a couple of times, air hoses had snapped. All in all, it was an irascible group that finally got to Lakewood. On arrival there, I was greeted by a Maine reporter who took a sneering view of the whole affair.

"So who's coming from Hollywood?" he said. "Who you got? Who's important?"

"Sam Mitnik for one," I snapped, pulling a name out of the humidity. "Does that satisfy you?"

The reporter was impressed. "Mitnik, himself? Say, that's worth a story!"

Sam was booked immediately as a guest of honor at the premiere. It was his debut in the world of banquets and headlines. To make it easy for him, I sent a wire to the head table at the climactic moment.

"Important merger pending. Regret unable to attend. Flying to London. Mitnik."

Since then, Sam has been borrowed at one time or another by every studio in Hollywood and has registered for every important premiere, conference or junket on the books. His telegram of regrets always arrives at the crucial moment and it might be from Paris or it might be from Peru. Sam gets around.

He has been paged for hours in Texas hotels. He has been

scheduled on Chicago radio and television programs. He has broken appointments at Miami Beach. Head tables have awaited him all the way from California fish joints to the Waldorf Astoria. Private cars have stood with their motors running, waiting for Mitnik to dash up and jump in. Hotel managers have suffered apoplexy, wondering who's going to pay the bar checks signed by Sam.

He once promised to show up with a delegation of Boy Scouts. He used to be an Eagle Scout, naturally. 'Merit Badge' Mitnik, his intimates call him.

He sent his usual telegram, of course. This time it came from Washington where he said he was dickering with the Government in an effort to buy the Pentagon. Sam said he wanted it for a rest home for all frustrated phonies outside of Boston who claim to have known him . . . or invented him.

But . . . such is fame. Now—according to the latest reports—Sam Mitnik has been claimed by the Russians.

THE STORY OF THE EXCOMMUNICATED MIDGETS

"THIS IS Walter J. Minton calling."

Thus, a voice greeted me on the other end of the phone.

"So?" I answered.

"Dick Lederer of Warner Brothers told me to contact you. I'm calling you from my office in New York."

"Oh, yeah?" said I.

Now, whyinhell would anyone at Warner Bros. tell someone to call me long distance, especially after I "retired" from their active payroll? It made no sense.

"I'm with G. P. Putnam, the book publishers. Obviously, my name doesn't mean anything to you."

"To tell you the truth, Mister, it doesn't."

"I *am* G. P. Putnam," the voice shouted emphatically.

133

"Warner Brothers has an option on a book which we have published. We are looking for someone like yourself to handle the promotion."

Now a rib is a rib. I have been called by Churchill, Christine Keeler and an assortment of "big names," also by schlmeils who think it is funny to identify themselves as someone else.

"It's your nickel," I said.

"The book is called *The Bramble Bush*," Minton continued. "It is a story of New England and what goes on in the summertime on Cape Cod. Lederer told me that you were the best man we could get to handle this sort of publicity. If you are interested can you meet with me at my office in New York tomorrow morning?"

I am not that kind of shmuck to hop on a plane to make a visit to New York just because someone calls me and asks me to.

I checked with Dick Lederer. He confirmed that Minton's call was genuine. I phoned Mr. Minton back. This was his story:

"We hired Jim Moran, the famous publicist to promote the book. Now, Jim has a quirk in his brain . . . something about using midgets wherever possible. He hired two lilliputians, made a huge enlargement of the title page of *The Bramble Bush* and sent them to Fall River to the home of the Bishop. The idea was to have the Bishop ban the book since it depicted a Catholic priest in a derogatory manner.

"When the Bishop saw what foolishness was afoot, he threw the midgets out of his home and excommunicated them." (If anyone needs two excommunicated midgets, I know where to get them.)

"It seems that Moran is a good gag-type publicist. Our book was no gag. Now, Warners doesn't want to make a picture out of the book until it becomes a best seller. Moran has loused us up. We want someone to take up the promotion of the book and get it on the right track."

I was quick to realize that Walter Minton was in a bind.

"What do you think you can do for us?" Minton asked.

In my business you have to come up with ideas at the drop of a hat. In this case, at the drop of a book.

I outlined what I thought was a pretty good campaign.

"I'd like to see the book banned," I finished.

"So would I," Minton said. "But they don't do things like that anymore!"

We talked some more. Minton agreed to let me handle the promotion *if* I could produce some of the seemingly-impossible ideas I had outlined. After all, Moran the Great had bamboozled them once. They didn't want another dud in me.

As I left Minton handed me a book. "Take this to your wife. If she likes to read something 'offbeat' she may enjoy it. It's a book which my associate picked up from Olympia Press in Paris. We don't know whatinhell it's all about. See what your wife thinks of it."

I looked at the title. It was one word—an unfamiliar one— *Lolita*.

I returned to Boston wondering where to start. A good fee was forthcoming if I could make New Englanders aware of *Bramble Bush,* a story of euthanasia and fornication on Old Cape Cod.

I went to my friend Hal Clancy, managing editor of the *Boston Traveler*. On my way over to his office I had an idea.

The first lesson in publicity-planting is to make a story sound newsworthy.

I telephoned the head of the Cape Cod Chamber of Commerce, Norman Cook. He is a hale and hearty fellow, best described as "a nice guy." I told him I was publicizing a book about the Cape and that it was loaded with nothing but wife-swapping and sex. Would he indignantly tell a newspaper reporter that such happenings were figments of an author's imagination? That such a story discourages visitors from coming to the Cape during the summer?

"Cripes, all they do on the Cape is screw," he chuckled. "You wouldn't want me to lie, would you?"

"Yes, I would," I said.

"Okay, for you I will," Norm laughed.

With tongue in cheek, I told Hal Clancy that Warners wanted to make a film out of *The Bramble Bush* but that the book was too suggestive and sexy and that censors were determined to stop it from becoming a motion picture. Hal called in a news reporter, Charles Ball.

"Charley, Art thinks he has a story about a motion picture and a book with a New England locale. See if you can get something out of it."

After a few minutes of questioning Ball shrugged his shoulders. "You don't have a goddam story. This is a lot of crap and you know it. What's the angle?"

Tell the truth to a newspaperman and you will never go wrong. (As a fourth-estater myself I knew that once you try to "con" a reporter you'll never do it again.)

"*You* know that there's no story here," I started, "and *I* know there's no story here, but before I leave I'll have a great one for you."

"You've got ten minutes. Then I go to lunch," Charley said.

"Suppose I tell you that the head of the Cape Chamber of Commerce wants this book kept out of every bookstore and library on the Cape. Would that be a story?"

"It might," Charley admitted. "But will he say it?"

I called Norm Cook again.

"Norm," I crossed my fingers. "I'm here at the *Boston Traveler* with Charley Ball, the reporter, who wants to get a statement from you about *The Bramble Bush.* . . ."

136

"What? That crap, again?" Norm shouted. "What in hell am I supposed to say?"

I paused for a moment and gasped. "Repeat that again!" I yelled.

"Repeat what?"

"Tell Charley what you just said to me. You called *Bramble Bush* 'another Peyton Place'?"

Charley looked up from the funny section of the *Traveler*.

"What did he say? Did I hear you correctly? Norm called it 'another Peyton Place'?"

"That's right," I lied. "Here ask him."

I got on an extension phone and repeated my question to Norm. "Tell Charley, Norm, he's on the other phone. Repeat what you said about *Bramble Bush*."

Angrily, Norm came through: "Whoinhell are these so-called 'experts' who write about the Cape and talk about fornication, adultery, incest and other vices? My job is at stake. I'm going on record to say that *The Bramble Bush* is an insult to Cape Cod and its year 'round residents and tourists who flock here from all over the world. It's nothing more than ribald, obscene and shocking! It's another 'Peyton Place' and should not be read by anyone with an iota of decency."

I watched Charley taking notes. He kept muttering: "Yes, Mr. Cook. Yes, Mr. Cook."

"He certainly is mad," Charley grinned.

Before leaving I casually dropped a photograph of the author, Charles Mergendahl, Jr., a native Bostonian, on his desk.

The following day, the lower half of the *Boston Traveler* bore a screaming eight column headline, "Boston Author pens another Peyton Place." The story had a photograph of the author, Charles Mergendahl, Jr. Norm Cook was quoted in detail. Charley Ball had his first by-line story.

The next day I called the Mayor of New Bedford, Francis Lawler. He was a good friend of mine. I had once arranged for him to appear for a bow on the Ed Sullivan Show.

Frank wouldn't order the banning, per se, of *Bramble Bush*. He suggested that he could have his City Solicitor draw up a legal complaint which would result in a fine and arrest of book sellers displaying the book. This would serve the same purpose. I also called Mayor Mel Morrison of Dover, New Hampshire. Mel agreed to help, too. So did Charley Lewin, the great guiding genius of the *New Bedford Standard Times* and *Cape Cod Standard-Times*.

Within a few days my stories appeared in Boston, New Bedford, Cape Cod and Dover. The story was carried throughout the nation by wire services. *Bramble Bush* started to make its appearance on "the charts" of best-selling books. The ultimate was achieved. It became the number-one best selling book in the *New York Times* book section. Warner Bros. purchased the motion picture rights.

A year later, Oscar Dystel, head of Bantam Books, called me. "I heard from Walter Minton of Putnam's what a great job you did for him with *The Bramble Bush*. We have the paperback rights. Do you want to help us push it?"

I accepted the challenge. What happened?

"Read it! Burn it!" shouted the legend on the back of the paperback. Dystel was satisfied. So was I. The cheaper edition of *The Bramble Bush* hit a record-breaking sale of four million copies.

Just before the movie of *Bramble Bush* was released, Oscar Dystel called me again. "Have you heard about Charley Mergendahl?"

"What happened?" I asked.

"He's dead! He was just found on the bottom of his cellar stairs. He evidently tripped on the top step and was lying dead in the cellar for hours before his body was discovered."

Charles Mergendahl, Jr.'s life was replete with tragedy. Early in their marriage his wife had died of cancer leaving a daughter six years old.

Bramble Bush, his first novel, hit the jackpot. He never lived to see it on film. The moving hand writes and having writ moves on.

MORAN OR MIRAGE?

LEGENDS ABOUT Jim Moran are legion. Whether he is real or not is a matter of conjecture among fellow press agents. Like Sam Mitnik, he may be somebody's pipe dream.

Stories have it that Moran (if he really exists) got his first claim to fame when he sold refrigerators to Eskimos. This made him the original "Noodnick of the North." His exploits have been documented far and wide. Someone with a beard appeared on the Jack Paar TV Show and claimed he was Jim Moran. He was a weird-looking, incoherent codger who told about the lurid pranks he had perpetrated on his clients. But even Jack Paar wasn't sure.

It has been said that press and press agents go together, like the two sides of a counterfeit coin, like Romulus and Remus sucking from the same fiendish tit. Or that a press agent is one who takes in lying for a living. Whatever you think of them, Moran typifies the more highly successful "screwball" publicist.

Some of Jim's so-called publicity stunts include an idea to cross a turkey with a centipede in order to obtain an incalculable number of turkey legs. Since the idea was thought of during a wartime meat shortage, it was given much free newspaper space.

Jim presumably was once a Warner Bros. publicist. As one mad wag reported: "You get your basic training as a publicist at Warner Bros. Once you've worked for them in publicity, you've learned everything in the book of tricks." It seems nearly anyone of contemporary literary importance worked for Warners at one time or another. (Reginald Rose and David Susskind are but two examples.) You can compare the racket to working in a whorehouse. If you get fired you just pack up your douche bag and typewriter and latch onto some other "house."

Moran's other familiar and not-so-familiar gags include:

Hatching a bay ostrich egg in twenty-three days to publicize a movie *The Egg And I*. He named it Ossip Moran.

When his landlady refused to paint the outside of a small Hollywood cottage in which he resided during his "lean" years (it is said that Jim weighs well over 225 pounds, now), he painted ten-foot high letters on the side of his residence. When viewed from a distance they spelled a four-letter Anglo-Saxon word, commonly used by Henry Miller. Needless to add, the landlady promptly painted the domicile and destroyed Moran's outdoor billboard.

He entered a Hollywood art contest for modern painting. He signed it "Naromji," which was "Jim Moran" jumbled up. The crazy-mixed-up painting was listed among the first five winners. Moran says he later sold it to Madman Muntz, an automobile dealer, for $750.

He ran for the Senate in California in 1946. He got 20,000 votes with the slogan: "What this country needs is a good five cents."

He developed a "Fatolator," a machine designed to render fat out of the air. He contended that since many people are on diets these days, their fat must be going somewhere. He concluded that it was in the atmosphere.

The Fatolator was about the size of a one-suiter case and was fitted with wheels and gears and lights. Its purpose was

140

to get the fat out of the atmosphere. He demonstrated its use on a Dave Garroway television show one morning. After turning on the machine, a whisper of smoke emitted from the case. A chime sounded and the machine stopped. Moran then opened the drawer and produced a tiny ball of fat, about the size of a walnut. Garroway promptly weighed himself.

He came to staid Boston and placed ads in all the newspapers looking for twelve men: two nearsighted, two farsighted, two bleary-eyed, two bright-eyed, one with an astigmatism, one cross-eyed, and two with 20–20 vision. He dressed the nearsighted, farsighted and normal men in Colonial uniforms, and the rest in British uniforms. Moran equipped himself in the uniform of a Colonial colonel. He gave his troops muskets and blank bullets and for two days drilled them on the Boston Common in full view of benchwarmers and local bums. He was out to prove that: "Don't fire until you see the whites of their eyes!" was the stupidest command in the history of warfare." The cross-eyed, astigmatic and 20–20 visioned men fired all over the lot missing one another. Moran was then in the employ of an eyeglasses manufacturer.

While working on a film *The Mouse That Roared,* Moran christened himself as James Sterling Moran, the Ambassador of Grand Fenwick, the mythical kingdom in the film. Much to the delight of philatelists he had specially-printed Grand Fenwickian stamps printed and distributed. Moran dressed himself in a handsome uniform, custom-made for his bulky frame and drove around Washington in a foreign-made limousine with a sterling silver mouse as a radiator design. He headquartered at the fashionable Hotel Shoreham. Diplomats flocked to his "party" and conned top Washington brass and VIP's into viewing the picture prior to its national release.

As a visiting Prince from Arabia, he frequented Ciro's, a popular Hollywood nitery, with a retinue of slaves. He would drop clever imitations of emeralds, rubies and diamonds all over the joint. Since it was below Moran's dignity to pick up these jewels Ciro's became a scene of bedlam as waiters, customers, musicians and busboys tried to retrieve the phony gems.

He engaged in raising a "furtle," a giant turtle with a coat of 'possum fur pasted to its shell. "I did it just to screw people up," says Moran.

He equipped two hundred homing pigeons with eyeglasses and treated them with a glass defogger called "X–M." "About 90 per cent of the X–M ones came home all right," says one student of Moranism. (I can imagine what someone thought when he picked up a stray homing pigeon wearing bifocals, looking for a place to perch.)

His fetish for surrounding himself with midgets is well known. Someone told me that he has organized a group called: "Moran Midget Employment Stabilization Board," since Jim feels that midgets have a very unstable unemployment problem. After all, how often does someone need a midget for a job? He once tried to launch a group of midgets flying on kites in Central Park. It was his intention to have these lilliputians hold advertising cards with messages on them. Unfortunately, the gendarmes of New York intervened and another Moran idea fizzled in mid-air.

A friend tells me that he attended Moran's monstrous apartment on West End Avenue in Manhattan where the publicist held forth with an oration on: "The Importance of the Flush Toilet in American Life," illustrating his erudite treatise with recorded sound effects of flushing toilets recorded in the men's room of the Library of Congress and on a moving train.

Does this guy Moran really exist? Who knows? But you've got to admit . . . it doesn't make a bad story!

THE WEALTHY PRINCESS OF JARPUTANA

IT WAS many months afterward when the Hindu Princess came to town. She was the daughter of a fabulously wealthy Maharajah, well educated and darkly beautiful, a lovely subject for the feature writers and photographers if her visit to Chicago had been nothing more than a stay between trains. But hers was no casual call. She had come on a definite and romantic mission. She wanted to give away a couple of million dollars.

She arrived without any preliminary notice and was met by no brass bands. She went to the Blackstone Hotel and established herself in a suite with seventeen trunks and a couple of dark brown body servants. Then she called the manager and asked him shyly if he had heard of a newspaper in the town called the *Tribune*. Sometime later a *Tribune* reporter visited her. When he went back to his office, he was dizzy.

The story of the Maharajah's daughter was stranger than truth. Many years ago there had been a sudden uprising in Jarputana, one of those quarrels between Mohammedans and Hindus. As revolutions go, it hadn't amounted to much because there aren't many Mohammedans in Jarputana. Eventually, His Britannic Majesty's troops had come through Lateekh Pass and established order. But while the fighting was going on the Maharajah suddenly found himself in a bad way. He had been on a journey far from his capital, unaware that trouble was in the offing, when a wandering band of revolutionaries surrounded the minor palace in which he had taken lodging and made preparations to kill him. In this desperate emergency he was saved by a young American engineer, who had been in the palace installing a waterworks or something. The American smuggled him through the rebel lines in a bedroll.

"And that is why I am here," said the Princess. "The American went his own way the next morning, refusing to accept any reward for what he had done. When peace had come and my father's power was assured once more, he had searches made for his rescuer all over India. But they were unsuccessful. We do not even know the name of this American. We know really nothing about him except that he mentioned to my father that his home was in Chicago in the United States of America. And we know also when he went away, he allowed my father to put a gold ring on his finger as a token of remembrance.

"My father, as you may have heard, died three months ago, and he willed that the eldest of his family come to America and look for this man. He meant my brother, but my brother died soon afterward and the task fell to me. My father's brave rescuer can identify himself with the ring and I shall deliver to him the two million dollars that my father wished him to have. I have heard of the Chicago *Tribune*. I feel you can help me to find him. . . ."

Maybe the story wasn't exactly like that . . . but you get the spirit of the thing. It was printed in the *Tribune* the next day with many interesting pictures.

It was a complete scoop. The *Examiner*, apparently, hadn't heard about the Princess. And it remained a scoop. For none of the afternoon newspapers that day carried a line about her. Managing Editor Edward Beck of the *Tribune*, who appears to have been out of town when the Maharajah's daughter called his office, returned to read the piece in puzzlement. It was just too good. He chased a reporter over to the Blackstone and received the heartening information that the

Princess and her seventeen trunks had departed. Then he hired a private detective to look into the matter while cables to the foreign service were failing to prove that any maharajah of the name mentioned by the Princess had recently died or, indeed, that any such potentate had ever existed. Presently, the detective reported:

"I can't find any trace of the girl or the servants. They went out of town on the *Century* to New York. But I got some dope on who rented the suite. . . . He was a one-eyed guy named Bowie."

Not so long after that a new moving picture came to Chicago. It was entitled *The Maharajah's Daughter*.

A DOGGONE SHAME

MANY A PRESS AGENT'S dreams are shattered when some mysterious element creeps into his well calculated plans. Like the time when Warner's sent a crew of press agents to handle the world premiere of a movie called *Goodbye, My Lady*. It starred Academy Award winner Walter Brennan along with Phil Harris, Brandon de Wilde . . . and a rare Basenji dog.

Goodbye, My Lady is the tender and touching story of an orphaned Mississippi swamp lad's love for a dog. A child whose simple goodness and ingrained sense of right and wrong sustain him through the heartbreak of surrendering a dog that doesn't belong to him.

It was only logical that the world premiere of the film should take place in Albany, Georgia, since the film's locale was *Mississippi*. Don't ask me why. I know of an instance where the Warner moguls insisted that *Moby Dick* be premiered in New London since one top executive thought it was a story about submarines. "Isn't New London the biggest submarine base in the East?" he asked.

It was agreed that one of the highlights of the premiere would be a dog show to be held in Albany's only hotel. The whole hamlet had a limited, peace loving population of about one thousand people.

World premieres were far and few between in this town. The hotel manager was reluctant to go along with this idea of a dog show, but agreed to it when he was promised free national newspaper stories. He also would house the principals in the film, which included Brennan and de Wilde, as well as a coterie of press agents from Warners.

"Instead of giving one prize for the best dog, let's give lots of prizes for the smallest, the biggest, the hairiest, the most bowlegged, the one with the biggest ears, the biggest teeth, etc. etc.," volunteered one of the press agents. So it was decided to ask everyone to bring in their dogs to vie for these innumerable prizes.

The next day people from neighboring Georgia towns as well as Albany, brought hundreds of mongrel and nondescript pooches into the hotel lobby. Confronted with this menagerie, the press agent threw up his hands and told the manager to give the prizes to whichever contestant he thought qualified under the vague rules of the contest. He quickly hopped a plane back to New York.

The next day a wire was received at Warner's New York office. It read: "Hotel lobby full of 235 stray dogs. What will we do?" It was signed by the manager of the hotel.

It seemed that those competing for prizes had rounded up any stray dog they could find. They brought them directly to the hotel. When the prizes—ten pairs of guest tickets to the local theatre "world premiere" and a total cash amount of twenty-five dollars—were dispersed, the "contestants" left their newly-found canine pets in the hotel lobby. Rumors have it that the rubber plants in the hotel won't need watering for the next three years.

146

WHAT'S UP, DOC?

DR. HARRY S. BERNSTEIN was one of my first clients. He was recommended to me by Harold Krensky, then an advertising solicitor for the Hearst newspapers. "Doc," as we called him, wanted me to plant a story in the newspapers that he had once transformed a Japanese into an American, during World War II. The only way you could tell that he was Japanese, according to Doc, was that somewhere on his body he had tattooed "Made In Japan."

It was my task to get the Doc publicity in newspapers for his plastic surgery business, which he conducted from a small Boston office. Harold placed his ads in the Hearst newspapers. No other papers would take them. They consisted of a photograph of the Doc with a celebrity. The caption would suggest by inference that the Doc had been bosom friends with the celebrity and that plastic surgery, of one form or another, was performed by him on this well-known person.

I would obtain the celebrity from the RKO Boston Theater where stage shows were once a weekly feature. Doc's ads usually ran in the *Sunday Advertiser*. Since the shows closed on a Tuesday, the publicity meant little or nothing to the performers. It did, however, build up the Doc's ego.

One afternoon I told the Doc to meet Harold and me backstage in the Green Room of the RKO Boston Theater. The celebrity was Jimmy "Schnozzle" Durante.

"Just keep your mouth closed," I told the Doc.

"We'll take the picture and then run like all hell to get it into the paper. If Jimmy asks you what it's for, tell him to talk to either me, Harold or Red King, the RKO press agent."

The Doc agreed.

Frankie Manchester, a member of the Hearst ad department who had been given a camera to cover important assignments such as this, was with us.

Jimmy came downstairs. We put him next to the Doc and just as Frankie began to focus his camera (which usually took twenty minutes to half an hour, Jimmy turned to the Doc and grumbled:

"What's de pitcher fer?"

Before anyone could answer, the Doc piped up: "Oh, I'm a doctor and . . ."

"A docter? What kinda docter?" Schnoz demanded.

"I perform plastic surgery on noses and . . ."

Before the Doc could finish his sentence Jimmy started to run around the room, holding onto his nose, screaming:

"Stop him! He's after me wid a knife!"

We finally managed to get Jimmy next to Doc and Frankie snapped his picture. It appeared in the *Sunday Advertiser*. It was the only picture I've ever seen of Jimmy where he looked *worried*.

TWO JACKS AND A JOKER

WHEN JACK DEMPSEY met Jack Sharkey for the world's heavyweight title, it was f(r)ought full of cries of "foul," by the Boston ex-sailor, who had become world's champion.

I first met Jack Dempsey and Jack Sharkey at a meeting of the Tub Thumpers of America, a gag society for press agents, of which I was the founder. I graciously posed with the two Jacks for a newspaper photographer.

I raised my hands and made a grimace, as the Manassa Mauler squared off with me. Sharkey acted as referee.

As the camerman clicked the shutter I shouted: "Foul!"

Sharkey didn't think this was funny. He picked me up by my coat lapels and bellowed: "What are ya, a wise guy or sumpin'?"

148

Dempsey stepped between us none too gently. "Aw, come on, Jack, let's not go through that routine again!"

The best hands of the day were a couple of jacks and I almost got them . . . right across the face!

VIVA, VORLDLY VOMAN!

OFTEN THE GREATEST planned press agent's stunts fall flat. Again, something unexpected may make the front page. Like the time that Col. Bill Hendricks of Warner Bros. decided to launch the old chestnut stunt of having a movie star "lose" her bathing suit while filming a scene. So, when Bill decided to have Virginia Mayo suddenly search for a missing shoulder strap to her skin-tight bathing suit, coincidentally, a battery of cameramen just "happened" to be on the beach, nearby. Papers throughout the land—and abroad, I might add—carried the "scoop" with proper credits to the Warner Bros. film in progress. You'd think that newspapermen would be wary of such press agent shenanigans.

Or the time that Eva Six, a bit player in American International's *Operation Bikini,* came out of her press clippings and was launched as a "Marilyn Monroe who speaks like Zsa Zsa Gabor." I took her to Harvard College to visit the *Crimson* newspaper office. She was squired by Joe Russin, one of the editors. He took her and a reporter and cameraman from the Hearst newspapers (who just "happened" to be with her) to view the historical scenes in the famous Yard.

A member of the college's *Student News* (the official publication of one sort or another—I still don't know of what) politely asked us all to leave and not take any photos in the Yard.

"Why?" I asked.

"Well, we wouldn't want John Harvard to show up in a

commercial or in an advertisement. It isn't dignified, you know," he said.

By this time the Hearst cameraman had already taken a picture of said Miss Six and a fellow Hungarian student. John Harvard was in the background, as big as life.

That afternoon, Loretta McLaughlin, a reporter on the Boston *Record-American* told a waiting world how Miss Six was "kicked out" of Harvard, and how rude Harvard men were. She bore out the truism that "you can always tell a Harvard man . . . but you can't tell him much!"

How did I feel? Wonderful!

I journeyed with Miss Six to Harvard's traditional New Haven rival, Yale. Here I obtained permission to visit indoors, and Miss Six posed with students, in particular one Pat Randolph, sitting on the traditional Ivy fence and standing beside the bird's haven, a statue of Theodorvs Woolsey, one of Yale's honored first presidents. The result?

The *New Haven Register* ran the story with an alluring MM-like photo of Eva on the steps of the coveted Sterling Library. She had been refused permission to dirty the granite stairs of the Widener Library at Harvard.

The story was headlined: "Yale Velcomes Vomanly Voman" and went on to say:

"Eva Six is a blonde, pleasantly talkative Hungarian refugee turned Hollywood actress.

"She possesses (along with many obvious attributes) an accent which is warmly captivating and easily understood . . . making her as easy on the ears as she is on the eyes.

"Her accent is unnoticeable in her first American film, *Operation Bikini*, which opens April 11 at Loew's College Theater." (This is the plug we wanted. The reporter could have stopped here and we would have been rewarded for the time and effort expended over a bowl of cold onion soup.)

"In the film she plays a Filipino guerrilla and her speaking part is in that language. However, her accent is probably the only thing about her that is unnoticeable.

"'Ve had to do remakes of some scenes,' she mused, 'because of the vay I valk.' It seems the directors cautioned her that guerrillas do not necessarily use the same body motion in walking that Miss Six uses.

"'But I can't help it if I viggle . . . I'm a vomanly voman and I viggle.' And she's right.

"Further, she has already been tabbed as a 'voluptuous vomanly voman.' And she is.

"As Miss Six discloses this information she stares directly into the eyes (gulp) of the person to whom she is speaking. (Hers are dark brown.)

"Anyhow, Miss Eyes, oops, rather Miss Six will have starring roles in (and she rattled off some new films for AIP and a TV series)." I was rather skeptical that either would be made, so it remains to be seen that, after all of these months, whether her prophesy came true.

The article went on to relate:

"As she downed a dish of strawberries and whipped cream, she announced: 'I don't have to vatch my veight—it's in my contract to remain voluptuous.'

"Closer examination showed (1) it's a good contract; (2) she's living up to it, and (3) on her it looks good.

"Born Eva Klein, she became Eva Kennedi (a likely story) during the 1956 Hungarian revolt. Subsequently she was Eva Mezel while acting in Budapest, then Eva Schmidt when she married Roy Schmidt.

"'I vass alvays knows as "Sunshine,"' she confessed, 'so Eva Six became my sixth name and it has six letters—Eva Six, see??' (Yes, eye see—whew those eyes are really dark brown.)

"Her week end in New Haven climaxed a trip through New England publicizing her film. 'You know,' she said, 'I

151

vas banned in Har-ward.' (It was felt the movie people were going to make commercial use of Widener Library.)

"But Yale accepted her! Saturday afternoon she made a tour of the Eli campus under scrutinized eyes. Unfortunately, most of the student body was on vacation and the Blues missed her brown eyes.

"Before leaving, Eva said, 'I do not vant to be known because Six sounds like sex (eye to eye again); I'd rather be known for my Six-cess as an actress.'

"Vell . . . at least she made it a 'six-cessful' week end for the Elis, for when she left town the final score was Yale Six, Harvard 0."

FIRED WITH ENTHUSIASM

A STORY which has seldom been told is the one about one of Hollywood's greatest moguls, the last of the patriarchs in the movie mecca. One of his brothers, in his later years, was always accompanied by a secretary whose sole duty was to zip up his fly whenever he came out of the "john."

Our movie pioneer is sort of a clown-prince-of-Hollywood. He is the recipient of innumerable medals, awards and citations. One newsreel showed him out of step receiving a high French award, taking it with his right hand and saluting with his left. Rumors have it he was a high ranking officer in the U.S. Air Force but had to give up flying planes (because his elastic broke). Whatever the reason, the story among top echelon is that his wife was a notorious nymphomaniac. He hired three of his best friends, all trusted studio employees, to spy on her. They "bugged" her rooms with tape recorders, took movies of her nocturnal activities with infra-red lights and had a dossier on her escapades which they gave to Mr. Big, daily.

Such loyalty from true friends was cherished by him.

One day while riding around in his imported car on the curves of Italy, he failed to negotiate a turn and as the sun blinded him, temporarily, he crashed into the mountainside. Hospital attendants and doctors said he couldn't live for more than a week or maybe a month. His unfaithful wife flew to his bedside. As he regained consciousness he looked at his wife for forgiveness and said: "If I ever come out of here alive, dear, I'll promise you anything."

"Anything?" she coyly teased him.

"Yes, anything!" he sobbed.

"Good, then I want you to promise to put my son-in-law in as head of the studio and fire your three faithful ones. I know they have been spying on me. Is that a promise?" she asked.

"Yes, yes," he sighed. "But stay with me until I get well."

"Sign this first," she said as she handed him a document.

As if by a miracle, he recovered and returned to Hollywood none the worse for the accident, physically, that is. His wife produced the document which set forth the "conditions" he promised on his death bed.

He called in his three wise men, and one by one he told them he had to fire them. He elevated his son-in-law, the lowly, once-handsome, part-time actor to head of the studio. He had kept his promise. He had no choice. Word went out that the three hirelings were out of work and that no studio was to "touch them." They collected their unemployment checks weekly. Then payments ceased. Calls to Mr. Movie Mogul went unanswered. Two of Mr. Big's cohorts "retired" for good.

Then one day, word got out that a big "Nixon for President" movement was being headed by this same Hollywood mogul.

One of our three wise men waited for him and confronted

him with: "Well, C.J., I understand you are campaigning for Nixon and that you will be head of his committee from the film capital. I have records and proof that you asked me and others to spy on your wife. We have photographs to prove it, too. Now, I think the magazines and newspapers would like this material, don't you?"

Mr. Big almost had a stroke. "But, you are my friend!" he shouted.

"Friend, you say? With you for a friend I don't need an enemy," countered his trusted ex-employee.

"What do you want of me?" he asked.

"I want my job back, that's all. And I want it back Monday morning. I'm flat broke, hungry and destitute, all on account of your whoring wife and your yellow spine!"

"Okay, you'll have your job back. Come to the studio gate on Monday morning at nine-thirty and you'll have instructions where to report. When you get your job, give me back those photos. Okay?"

Monday morning our man went to the main gate. His name was there as promised. He was asked to report to the personnel office. As he walked up the stairs to get his New assignment . . . he dropped dead!

Then there was the time that "Crazylegs" Hirsch, that great professional Rams' football player was on tour with me to publicize his film *Unchained*. (The picture flopped but the theme song went on to great heights.)

We went to a nightclub and met a voluptuous blonde movie star, who was also making a series of personal appearances all by herself. She had no press agent, no attendant, nobody was there to squire her except the local press agent who didn't know his ass from beans. She was a movie queen of much stature, who had incurred the wrath of a studio head to whom she was under contract. An ingenious plot was concocted to have her removed from the company's payroll. She was sent on an extensive coast-to-coast circuit, more than twenty-five cities in three months.

They convinced her that she was so smart that she didn't need any studio representative to accompany her on her whirlwind tour.

The actress took off and did a great job. She was good copy wherever she went. She not only publicized her film but the studio and entire motion picture industry as well. She served as sort of "Ambassador-of-Goodwill, without portfolio."

One day, towards the end of the tour, the actress got a call from her agent.

"It's all over," he wailed. "These sonsovbitches knew that when they sent you off on this trip alone that you'd forget that an option was coming up. That was three weeks ago. In your excitement you forgot to sign it. You're fired . . . finished . . . sweetheart. There's nothing anyone can do now!"

In Hollywood this is still considered a masterpiece. Not only did they get rid of the actress without too much effort and feuding, she had built up the picture's gross to astronomical figures and it didn't cost them a cent!

I was with "Crazylegs" the night she got the call. She didn't break down and cry. She took the money they gave her and now is one of the nation's wealthiest realtors in California.

"Movies ain't what they usta be," she philosophizes.

Then, how about the press agent who was promised that he would head up Warner Bros. publicity department because he did such an outstanding job for one of its great producers? When he finished his chores on a Friday afternoon, and returned to his office, to gather up his mail, which had been left unopened for three weeks due to his activities "on location" in below-freezing weather, he was greeted by a teletype which read:

"No reflection on your great ability. You have always done a great job, but your services are terminated as of today since we are embarking on a campaign of economy rather than energy. Regards (Signed) Head of the Publicity Department."

A teletype, yet! Something that everyone in the office could see. Was there no pride among the leaders?

How do I know? I still have the teletype to prove it!